MW01205037

Praise for *Inside the Minds*

"What C-level executives read to keep their edge and make pivotal business decisions. Timeless classics for indispensable knowledge." - Richard Costello, Manager of Corporate Marketing Communication, General Electric

"Want to know what the real leaders are thinking about now? It's in here." - Carl Ledbetter, SVP & CTO, Novell, Inc.

"Priceless wisdom from experts at applying technology in support of business objectives." - Frank Campagnoni, CTO, GE Global Exchange Services

"Unique insights into the way the experts think and the lessons they've learned from experience." - MT Rainey, Co-CEO, Young & Rubicam/Rainey Kelly Campbell Roalfe

"A must-read for anyone in the industry." - Dr. Chuck Lucier, Chief Growth Officer, Booz-Allen & Hamilton

"Unlike any other business books, *Inside the Minds* captures the essence, the deep-down thinking processes, of people who make things happen." - Martin Cooper, CEO, Arraycomm

"A must-read for those who manage at the intersection of business and technology." - Frank Roney, General Manager, IBM

"A great way to see across the changing marketing landscape at a time of significant innovation." - David Kenny, Chairman & CEO, Digitas

"An incredible resource of information to help you develop outside the box..." - Rich Jernstedt, CEO, Golin/Harris International

"A snapshot of everything you need to know..." - Larry Weber, Founder, Weber Shandwick

"Great information for both novices and experts." - Patrick Ennis, Partner, ARCH Venture Partners

"The only useful way to get so many good minds speaking on a complex topic." - Scott Bradner, Senior Technical Consultant, Harvard University

"Must-have information for business executives." - Alex Wilmerding, Principal, Boston Capital Ventures

www.Aspatore.com

Aspatore Books is the largest and most exclusive publisher of C-level executives (CEO, CFO, CTO, CMO, partner) from the world's most respected companies and law firms. Aspatore annually publishes a select group of C-level executives from the Global 1,000, top 250 law firms (partners and chairs), and other leading companies of all sizes. C-Level Business Intelligence™, as conceptualized and developed by Aspatore Books, provides professionals of all levels with proven business intelligence from industry insiders – direct and unfiltered insight from those who know it best – as opposed to third-party accounts offered by unknown authors and analysts. Aspatore Books is committed to publishing an innovative line of business and legal books, those which lay forth principles and offer insights that when employed, can have a direct financial impact on the reader's business objectives, whatever they may be. In essence, Aspatore publishes critical tools – need-to-read as opposed to nice-to-read books – for all business professionals.

Inside the Minds

The critically acclaimed *Inside the Minds* series provides readers of all levels with proven business intelligence from C-level executives (CEO, CFO, CTO, CMO, partner) from the world's most respected companies. Each chapter is comparable to a white paper or essay and is a future-oriented look at where an industry/profession/topic is heading and the most important issues for future success. Each author has been carefully chosen through an exhaustive selection process by the *Inside the Minds* editorial board to write a chapter for this book. *Inside the Minds* was conceived in order to give readers actual insights into the leading minds of business executives worldwide. Because so few books or other publications are actually written by executives in industry, *Inside the Minds* presents an unprecedented look at various industries and professions never before available.

INSIDE THE MINDS

Consulting Leadership Strategies

Industry Leaders on the New Benchmarks for Success

BOOK IDEA SUBMISSIONS

If you are a C-level executive or senior lawyer interested in submitting a book idea or manuscript to the Aspatore editorial board, please email authors@aspatore.com. Aspatore is especially looking for highly specific book ideas that would have a direct financial impact on behalf of a reader. Completed books can range from 20 to 2,000 pages – the topic and "need to read" aspect of the material are most important, not the length. Include your book idea, biography, and any additional pertinent information.

SPEAKER SUBMISSIONS FOR CONFERENCES

If you are interested at giving a speech for an upcoming ReedLogic conference (a partner of Aspatore Books), please email the ReedLogic Speaker Board at speakers@reedlogic.com. If selected, speeches are given over the phone and recorded (no travel necessary). Due to the busy schedules and travel implications for executives, ReedLogic produces each conference on CD-ROM, then distributes the conference to bookstores and executives who register for the conference. The finished CD-ROM includes the speaker picture with the audio of the speech playing in the background, similar to a radio address played on television.

INTERACTIVE SOFTWARE SUBMISSIONS

If you have an idea for an interactive business or software legal program, please email software@reedlogic.com. ReedLogic is especially looking for Excel spreadsheet models and PowerPoint presentations that help business professionals and lawyers achieve specific tasks. If idea or program is accepted, product is distributed to bookstores nationwide.

Consulting Leadership Strategies

Industry Leaders on the New Benchmarks for Success

CONTENTS

John R. Burgess   9
ENSURING CONSULTING SUCCESS

Gregg M. Steinberg   19
MAKING THE MOST OF YOUR PEOPLE

David W. Kenny   25
PROVIDING CLIENTS WITH REAL VALUE

Jeff Stewart   33
KEYS TO CONSULTING SUCCESS

Emad Rizkalla   41
*OVER-SATISFACTION: THE NEW CURRENCY
OF CONSULTING*

Phil Friedman   57
*MAINTAINING PROFITS AND SUCCESS IN A
CHANGING INDUSTRY*

Doug Gorman   67
*UNDERSTANDING CLIENT NEEDS AND
DELIVERING RESULTS*

Carla O'Dell   **77**
MEETING THE CHALLENGES OF THE
CONSULTING INDUSTRY

Mark Agustin   **83**
LEADING BY EXAMPLE

J. Wayne Gudbranson   **89**
KEY STRATEGIES FOR GROWING YOUR
BUSINESS

Steve Bloom   **101**
SUCCESS IS THE ONLY OPTION

Ensuring Consulting Success

John R. Burgess

Founder and Managing Director

International Profit Associates

Consulting companies need activity to succeed. Because closing rates are relatively modest, it is important that a consulting company's strategy includes a great deal of activity. We need a huge number of client contacts in order to maximize our likelihood of getting beyond our breakeven points.

At International Profit Associates, we use a tripod method of marketing that differentiates us in the market and helps us lock in clients. With this method, the initial contact with the client obligates the client to nothing other than a conversation. The second contact hopefully impels the client to believe they should have an analysis of their business. This analysis is offered at a very modest cost, so the client can determine whether there are in fact areas of the business that require remedial action. The third contact with the client subsequent to that analysis occurs when the client determines the remedial action should be executed and that they should hire us in order to effectuate the remedy. By using the tripod approach, we dramatically reduce the clients' concern that management consultants as a whole are too expensive relative to the perceived benefit.

Growing Profits by Growing Team

To ensure growing revenues, we can increase numerical counts across the board in each one of those three tripods areas at any given point in time. It is important that we have a team of well-trained and productive consultants in order to make these increases. We constantly train and retrain preexisting and new people. Preexisting people are retrained so we can increase our percentage probability, while it is necessary to hire and train new people so we can continue to build the core of the company. Statistically, over the past thirteen years we have found that once we meet with a client, there is a likelihood of success in obtaining the business. Therefore, by increasing the number of people we come into contact with as a well-trained and effective firm, we are almost certain to increase our revenue.

Costs and Revenue Limitations

The challenge of this business, or any other for that matter, is making a profit. Of course, the largest expense for our business is payroll. Second to that is travel. The perpetual cost of marketing is relatively high, and coupled with those costs is the fact that the type of clients we handle—small- and medium-sized businesses—have limited assets. In a perfect world, if the clients had more capability, such as more liquid assets, it would be relatively simplistic to continue to drive the revenue dramatically higher. Because the clients have finite assets, it means it is more difficult to increase the average sale price at any given point in time. The cap on our prices is not precipitated by us or by our experience, but rather it's determined by the client's ability to pay.

Training Focus

I spend between thirty and thirty-five out of the fifty-two weekends a year retraining. We provide regular retraining in order to sharpen existing skills and acquire new skills, both from the hierarchy of the company as well as from the individual employees who have developed new insights on maximizing the benefit to the client.

Our training sessions can consist of modest-sized groups of ten people to larger gatherings of many hundreds. We bring them together for an open, frank, and active discussion regarding skills and strategies to maximize the benefit the client receives, both from the analysis process and the consultancy process. We also discuss the state of marketplaces in which we work, because consultancy obviously has to be modified based on the overall economic activity.

Ensuring Success

We manage by the minute. You can't manage what you don't know, so our management methodology includes releasing hourly reports. Each department produces an hourly report stating how they did that given hour, not only in relationship to the goal quota, but also in relationship to how they did in previous hours that day, that week, and that year. At any given point in time, one can determine how individual units of the company are doing.

We measure success based on the amount of benefit we deliver to the client, which is the only logical way for any company to measure success. Of course, we also have to measure profitability and revenues, but a company only gets the opportunity to have good continuous numerics in those areas if they have a good product.

We monitor productivity success using the key numbers throughout the company in each department. To ensure quality service, senior executives monitor core groups, and consulting service directors monitor the benefit being delivered to the client on a daily basis.

Industry Changes

Since September 11th, people have been less inclined to invest time and money in their business, and are more interested in maintaining the status quo. During the Reagan and Clinton administrations, people were convinced there was a better tomorrow than today. At the moment, our perception is that tomorrow will be the same as today. This view extends to the economy, and potential clients are less likely to invest in demonstrative action to remedy any difficulties that might exist within their given models. However, I think that in the next five to ten years, people's perceptions will again change, and they will decide to get back to being competitive.

Ensuring Client Satisfaction

The golden rule of any business is absolutely treating each individual opportunity as if it were the only opportunity, regardless of its size or conditions. Today's opportunity is more important than any other. From that positive and focused attention will come better service, which results in activity and higher numbers.

Obtaining New Customers in the Consulting Industry

On a weekly basis, we hold management meetings in which we dissect our current strategy for client procurement and then determine what modifications we can make, if any, in order to increase our numbers. We calculate return on investment by determining the actual fixed and semi-fixed costs associated with each new model and the revenue that is actually produced based on that change, utilizing all variables. It is not possible to precisely identify the exact potential revenue source.

Competition

We don't believe we have any competition. We believe the only competition we have is ourselves. I think every company should manage itself this way. If you start worrying too much about what the competition does, inevitably you lose track of what you do well. The truth is that every business has to figure out how to be successful itself. It should each focus on its own goals and objectives, and on making modifications in its strategies to increase the odds of actually reaching those goals and objectives.

Merger and acquisition activity theoretically does not affect our market. What it would affect is the core of people that work here. If another company were to be capable of providing the same opportunities to their employees as we can, then of course it's possible that some of our people might feel the grass is greener on the other side of the fence. The concern we would have is if someone were to actually get to the point of being competitive with us, then of course that might change our sphere of influence as it relates to our key employees.

Creating Opportunities for Client Acquisition

We continue to increase the types of services we offer to the client. By increasing the service offerings, we hope to increase the average revenue per sale. In order to increase that average, however, we have to take into consideration the client's ability to actually compensate us for that. When adding products, we have to remain aware that we can only actually achieve a certain level of revenue from each individual client based not on what we're capable of delivering or achieving for the client, but based on the client's ability to afford the various products.

Challenges

Our biggest challenge in acquiring new clients is their lack of liquidity. The average entrepreneur in America starts out their business in a shoebox. They start their business because their perception is that they are better at what they are doing—say electrical contracting—than was their former boss. That doesn't make them a businessperson though. That makes them an electrician. The reality is that it takes them a very lengthy period of time to actually make business. In most instances—85 or 90 percent of the time —they never truly get to the point of being eminently successful and accumulating liquid wealth. As a result, they have very limited financial resources. Many times, they do not have the payroll for the week in hand on Monday morning, but rather have to generate it during that week. Often times, they do not have the financial wherewithal to actually do things they deem necessary and appropriate in order to drive their model higher. In some instances, such as buying equipment, as long as they have proper collateralization, they can obtain funding. They will not have adequate collateral to obtain funding for other expenditures, such as consulting. They know they need to invoke change, but unfortunately can't afford it. Therefore, they manage their business based on cash flow rather than profitability, and that is always the death knell of business. The business may not expire, but it will have a lack of success.

Long-term major increases in taxation from a small business perspective certainly would hurt us. Four or five years ago, the extraordinarily tight job market affected our business negatively. It was so tight that the clients could not obtain additional skilled workers, therefore putting themselves in a position where even if they were to fix their business, they had great concern that they would not actually be able to pull off the resolution.

The truth of the matter is that virtually all clients require assistance and outside intervention in order to remedy problems that exist within their businesses. Everyone in a lighter moment comes to the realization that there are methods and systems that could be employed in their business that would enhance their likelihood of success. However, the next issue is whether they are willing to commit the necessary resources, both monetary and in terms of time and resources, in order to remedy those problems.

Strategies for Acquiring New Clients

As mentioned earlier, we use a tripod methodology toward marketing where we pursue each individual client by establishing an initial appointment. In that appointment, we move on to the second leg of the tripod method, which involves the client agreeing to an analysis of business practices. The third leg is the client enlisting our implementation consulting.

We measure our success based on the financial success of our clients. Our client services department contacts every client immediately upon the completion of the consultancy. They try to get a clear understanding from the client as to their perception of the benefit received. If the benefit is not to the client's liking, we send someone back in to remedy the complaint.

Long-term relationships with clients are fostered by reinforcing with the client over a period of time that the benefit and the actual improvement were caused by only two factors. Those two factors are the client and us. The methods and systems we put into place are the reasons the client has dramatically improved profitability, cash flow, and ease of operation. If we do our job right, the client never needs us again for the specific issues they retained us for in the first place. If we do our job poorly, believe it or not, the client does need us again. The only time that's not a true statement is if the client has so increased their revenue base that the methods, systems, and controls we put into place when they were a $2 million company simply don't work for a $20 million company.

That's one of the major reasons we've added on new services. We actually have a tax division for small- and medium-sized businesses that have grown by over 100 percent a year for the last three years. We also have advisory and intermediary services where we advise people about the potential either of selling their business or of finding methodologies to limit the tax exposure on an estate planning basis if they die. We have these other adjunct products that allow us to maintain client relationships, even though the base consulting work generally means the client only needs our services once.

Tactical Support

Client service and tactical support are structured so there is an immediate response to any issues whatsoever that exist in the client's mind. If the client's perception is that something was done erroneously, then we immediately attack that issue head-on. We have to have a "the client is always right" approach, even though the client may be totally wrong.

Personal Contact

What client acquisition comes down to is, the companies that aggressively pursue the marketplace and find ways to increase the number of contacts they have with prospective clients that will increase their likelihood of success. Recently, some very large companies have had difficulty reaching their goals and objectives in various portions of the marketplace. They have then decided that those segments are no longer as viable for them and walked away. The reason they don't find success in those segments is because they never found a way to contact the market. You cannot contact the market through advertisement. You cannot contact the market through billboards. You cannot contact the marketplace by running an ad during the Super Bowl. A client's decision to change methods and systems for running the company does not come from reading a billboard. That decision comes from an intelligent, open, and frank discussion with another human being who can convince them there is a better way than that which is currently employed. What differentiates us from our competition is our willingness to have that face-to-face conversation. We have those discussions more than anyone else in our market.

John R. Burgess founded International Profit Associates (IPA) in Chicago in September of 1991, and has been the driving force behind IPA's success ever since.

IPA has become the largest management consulting company in the world, serving the needs of small- and medium-sized businesses—businesses in the United States and Canada that have revenues of $600,000 to $250,000,000.

In 2004, IPA had revenues of $195,000,000 and will surpass $200 million in 2005. No other management consulting company has reached $200 million in revenues from startup faster. In 2004, IPA was ranked by Consultant's News *as the fifty-sixth largest consulting company in the world for all types of businesses. In the fall of 2004,* Crain's Chicago Business *ranked IPA as the sixth largest management consulting company in Chicago.*

Throughout IPA's history, Mr. Burgess has provided the company with an ever-expanding vision to serve the needs of small- and medium-sized businesses. IPA has become for entrepreneurs the premier business development company in North America. Prior to founding IPA, Mr. Burgess was a commodities trader with the Chicago Board of Trade, practiced law in New York, and was an executive with another management consulting firm.

Mr. Burgess received a B.S. in business administration from Roger Williams College in Providence, Rhode Island, and a J.D. from the New England College of Law in Boston, Massachusetts.

Making the Most of Your People

Gregg M. Steinberg

President

International Profit Associates

As a service organization, the key assets of a consulting firm are the individual people that work within it. They are the force that delivers the knowledge transfer, creates client equity, and determines perceived brand image. Retention strategies are therefore critical as the means to ensure that key people stay with the organization. It is also critical to implement measures and standards within the organization to ensure that all the people who are delivering the product or service are able to do so with a consistently high quality. This control entails maintaining best practices in providing solutions to clients. The internal systems and controls, employee incentives, and continuing professional education programs must be clear and in place within each service or consulting organization, so each individual employee has access to and understands them.

Sales and Marketing

It is necessary to look at a business from both a standpoint of what's necessary to deliver quality service, and how to proactively handle the sales and marketing process. Many service organizations are reactive in their sales and marketing processes, and depend on their revenue to be generated by existing client relationships, referrals, or rainmakers. A firm needs to proactively control its sales and marketing productivity, rather than react to employees' individual sales efforts. Set agendas, goals, and quotas based on expectations of where the firm wants to be at any given point in time, and then drive a sales process to achieve that. This process is extremely proactive, in that field sales representatives and internal sales representatives directly contact potential clients, rather than relying on a narrow base of partner-level employees to produce the revenue. Drive the sales process down to the lowest common denominator within the organization so it's generating revenue within a broad base of people, rather than at the highest level. Essentially, a firm must turn the sales pyramid upside down and rely on many people to provide the revenue generation, rather than a few.

Monitoring Revenue and Profits

Although growing revenues and profits are aligned, they're not necessarily aligned in terms of what happens at the end of any given day. Driving revenue is a function of a sales and marketing process that identifies how many people are needed in order to achieve a certain revenue goal.

Determining the people necessary to achieve this goal is a formulary process. As an example, take a model that is very scalable in terms of how many salespeople, how many analytical consultants, and how many implementation consultants are needed. Develop a formulary process that can scale on a consistent basis, thus allowing the firm to drive the revenue to where it wants it to be, based on plugging certain human factors into those formulas. This is a key to a successful growth strategy; a business model must be scalable through various levels of the organization's maturation.

The profitability function is a combination of two factors. The first factor includes holding variable costs inline, tied directly to the revenue formula. It is incumbent on senior management to make sure the compensation, bonus, and incentive structures in place allow revenue to be driven to the desired result while keeping the highest quality of the services being delivered. The second piece of profitability is not allowing pure overhead expenses, recruiting expenses, and retraining expenses to get out of line as the company moves forward. Maintain strict controls on the overhead issues, tight proactive review, and consistent upward movement on the revenue numbers.

Managing Today While Planning for the Future

The main challenge to any organization is making sure the right formularies and day-to-day processes are in place to manage the company on an ongoing basis. When key matrices, benchmarks, trending ratios, and formularies are in place, running an organization on a daily basis becomes much more effective and efficient. Once those types of processes are in place, the challenges come more from looking at future growth opportunities and not allowing management's focus to get diverted into too many directions. Zero in on maintaining quality while entering into new service offerings. This involves identifying the right new service offering to put out to the market and making sure the people that are deployed to implement those services are trained at the highest possible level.

The Importance of Keeping Track

To keep on top of the business, it is necessary to track and trend key matrices within the company, not just on a monthly basis, but also on a daily basis, or even at various periods during the course of a day. Knowing what's going on within the organization as a whole and being able to identify problem areas before they rear their head is how a firm keeps its edge. Looking at specific operating data on a daily or hourly basis, depending on which spoke of the organizational hub is being considered, allows the firm to manage on a proactive basis. Measure hourly productivity goals by individual, manager, and department. Manage success by utilizing those numbers and formulas to manage the people at each of those levels. Everyone watches those measurement tools on an ongoing basis, so managers can address a problem before it becomes a problem.

Industry Changes

The industry has to be broken down into a couple of different areas. Ten years ago, the technology consulting component of the consulting industry was minimal compared to where it is now. The types of individuals that are recruited into consulting are dramatically affected by the nature and the type of consulting being done. Ten years ago, one could go to the B-schools and hire consultants for one type of firm, or go to senior mid-management people from the manufacturing or service sector for another type of firm. Those people could become consultants for a broad base of consulting firms doing strategy, operations, or sales and marketing work.

Now that technology consulting is driving a majority of the consulting revenue, a whole new breed of individuals needs to be recruited. Those people aren't necessarily coming out of the traditional places where consultants used to be found, and that fact has created its own set of challenges from a recruiting standpoint, as well as retention, work quality, and management standpoints. If the people who are now managing all these new consultants come from the old school, they are managing work they don't necessarily know how to do themselves.

On top of that, the sales and marketing piece—regardless of the nature of the work being delivered—has changed. Some of the old partnership models have changed. The rainmaker models have changed, and many firms have now gone to a direct sales effort versus a reactive sales effort.

In the years to come, there may be a continued movement towards more dedicated sales forces within the organizations. The firms that have grown from being pure strategy and operations firms to broadening out with service offerings across the board will excel. In order to do that and still retain their clientele and a competitive advantage with specific core competencies, they will be motivated to create more strategic alliances and joint ventures than before.

Pre-Requisites for Success

In any service organization, there are three requirements for success. First, there has to be a consistent quality of service delivery that aligns with the expectations of the client, both at the start of the project and throughout its implementation. This has to match with the ability to deliver on those expectations by the end of the project. Second, there has to be an organizational culture that is geared towards retention of the best employees. Third, there has to be a strong individual in control of both the top line and the bottom line in terms of aggressive revenue growth that's profitable and innovative.

Currently, Gregg Steinberg is president of numerous operating companies that, combined, form the largest consulting firm in the world; these companies deliver a broad spectrum of management consulting and other professional services solely to the small- and medium-sized business marketplace. The various entities are known in the marketplace as: International Profit Associates, IPA Advisory and Intermediary Services, Integrated Business Analysis (United States and Canada), International Tax Advisors, Creative Tax Strategies, IPA Professional Development Services, Accountancy Associates, ITA Implementation Services, and IPA Travel Services.

Mr. Steinberg's responsibilities include direct daily oversight of all the operating entities, management of the combined operations in terms of assuring that all companies are meeting short-term financial targets, as well as designing, developing, and implementing medium- and long-term strategic operational, financial, and growth objectives. Combined, the companies have over 1,800 employees throughout North America.

Mr. Steinberg joined IPA in 1992 (company revenues $5 million), became its chief financial officer in 1995 (company revenues $24 million), and took over as president in

1997 (company revenues $54 million). The company's 2003 annual revenue was $184 million, and 2004 revenues are anticipated to close in on $200 million.

Mr. Steinberg's affiliations and memberships include: Young President's Organization, American Management Association, Turnaround Management Association, Institute of Management Consultants, Association of Management Consulting Firms, National Association of Certified Valuation Analysts, Center for Entrepreneurial Management, and Birthing of Giants 99. Civic responsibilities include: past board member for Jewish Community Centers of Chicago, past board member and chairman for various committees of Jewish Council for Youth Services, current member of The Mankind Project, leadership roles with the Weizmann Institute for Science, and the Suburban Human Relations Commission.

Mr. Steinberg sat on the Board of The Quantum Group, Inc., and is currently a member of the United States Chamber of Commerce Small Business Council. Prior to joining IPA, he held various positions, including vice president of a hotel management company, president of a financial advisory firm, assistant director of mergers and acquisitions for a national investment banking firm, and director of corporate finance for a Chicago public accounting firm.

Mr. Steinberg is a graduate of the University of Arizona, with a bachelor's of science degree in business administration. He is also a graduate of The American Graduate School of International Management (Thunderbird), with master's degrees in international management and business administration.

Providing Clients with Real Value

David W. Kenny

Chairman and Chief Executive Officer

Digitas Inc.

Building Success through Relationships

Success in any service industry is contingent upon the ability to add sustained value to one's customers. Consulting—across the range of business services—is very much a service business, and any firm can simply complete a transactional project for a client. What differentiates a truly successful firm is that it develops extended relationships with its clients, through which the firm increasingly adds value over time, contributing to more than just one project and moving more deeply to the role of ongoing partner. These relationships are based on the firm having both a short- and long-term view of where the client is headed. Such relationships also depend on the firm's ability to offer practical and applicable advice and solutions. Consulting firms must be capable of delivering measurable top- and bottom-line results to their clients so they can prove how they have added value. The sustainable client relationship is the core to success in consulting.

Parallel to the sustainable relationship is fortitude of talent. A firm must develop loyal, capable employees over a long period of time. It is difficult to foster long-term client relationships if a firm cannot build long-term employee relationships. Employee retention and development is the foundation to developing an organization. The most successful organizations clearly articulate the role of the individual vis-à-vis company goals, client goals, and team goals. They also articulate paths of professional maturation and opportunity for all employees, regardless of level. And, finally, these organizations create merit-based rewards, recognition, and compensation opportunities that map to individuals' accomplishment of stated goals.

Achieving Growth at Digitas

Digitas is fundamentally a direct and digital marketing agency, so we assist our clients in using databases and the Internet to connect with their customers. Unlike most consulting firms that simply suggest solutions, we are equally and strongly focused to actually implement them. This combination of the practical and the visionary is what differentiates us; we make recommendations, we implement them, and we hold ourselves accountable for the results.

The basis of our revenue and profit generation lies in ensuring the growth of our existing clients. Each of our clients is assigned a relationship leader who is accountable for understanding what the client's challenges are and where their strategies and goals are headed. That clear understanding is essential to develop effective solutions that are central to our clients' success. Relationship leaders also build marketing engines that address clients' ongoing business and customer relationship goals. This approach allows us to contribute to the success of our clients by measuring the effectiveness of the programs we implement for them, and by building repeatable processes that allow them to manage and expand their customer relationships in real time across multiple media channels.

Of course, we also continue an ongoing set of discussions with potential new clients. Reputation and deep relationships allow us to identify companies that are likely to benefit from our approach to their work, and likewise, many of those same companies approach us to explore opportunities to help them. Initially, much of our work with new clients is seeded with projects, which when optimized over time become the deeper, ongoing partnerships that are the core of our business. In any given year, we expect half of our growth to come from the growth of our existing clients, and the other half to come from new ones.

The two main challenges in this industry are related. Fundamentally, the most demanding concern in consulting is finding talented people who are both practical and visionary. Talent is the core of any professional service firm. The first challenge is to retain the best and brightest people so they stay and grow with the company. The second related challenge is to make sure clients continue to invest in excellent talent as well. People cannot do their best work if they are not working with truly great companies and people. The best scenario is one in which the client company and consultant teams are considered as one. This optimizes learning, excellence, and nurturing, and it does a lot to cross-pollinate the attributes that make for successful individuals and companies.

Investing in the Client

The most expensive bet we make is in starting a new client relationship. Learning their business and teaching them ours requires a huge investment that can result in significant losses if the relationship does not work out. Therefore, we are very careful in our client selection.

We also work to keep our edge with respect to our customer base. I personally spend two-thirds of my time with clients. For keeping on top of my knowledge, there is simply no substitute for sitting down with senior clients and listening. A consultant advises clients with two ears and one mouth, and it is important to use them in that proportion. Without truly listening to what clients' problems and challenges are, there is no way to devise a viable solution to meet their needs.

At Digitas, we conduct semiannual strategic account reviews for every client. I meet with the teams that work with our clients and listen to how they perceive their progress. Our people generally know our clients very well and are articulate about their needs. These reviews allow me to set some priorities and draw from across the entire client base those themes that highlight where we might need to invest.

The Importance of Prioritizing

Making sure a company executes well really boils down to having clear priorities and effective metrics. Virtually all we accomplish is an initiative under one of three priorities. One of these is ensuring that every employee of Digitas achieves his or her full potential, an objective that is built upon a training, development, and mentoring agenda. We have metrics around retention rate, promotions, and execution that we monitor very closely.

Our second priority is making sure we are embedded and inextricably linked to our clients' marketing success. Our accomplishment in this objective is measured by how well our clients are doing in the marketplace, the status of their market share, and what percentage of the total marketing investment is related to matters we actually influence. Again, metrics are vital for this market share measure at a client level.

Our third priority is growth and development, so we have a metric to ensure that we improve on a yearly basis. Continuous improvement is a critical part of our business, and it may be the most difficult area to measure. We work to obtain clients' opinions on our innovation, which are very constructive because we must always be a step ahead. Creativity and innovation are critical to success. Have we led our clients to new ways of relating to their consumers that are fresh, novel, relevant, and effective?

Industry Changes

In the past, businesses employed outside researchers to obtain both data and an outside perspective. Now, the Internet has changed the accessibility and delivery of data in fundamental ways. As a result, the value is not in the data, but in interpreting it and basing practical suggestions on it. In addition, the world works much more quickly now. The old consulting model of collecting data, processing it, making recommendations, and implementing can no longer fit businesses' needs. We must come to conclusions very quickly, test them in the market, and improve on them all in real time. There is no longer a line between strategy and execution, so we must live in the business every day.

In the years to come, I predict that companies will continue to outsource to accomplish goals, whether they are strategy or marketing execution. The future difference: outsourcing will look, act, and be like partnering. Consulting firms will be a part of their clients' ecosystems, because it is much easier now to connect resources together. Outsourcing will extend to areas like information technology, finance and accounting, and human resources, so we will be more embedded in the businesses of our clients. We will be more operationally connected to them, as opposed to just doing think pieces on the side.

Choosing the Right Clients

At Digitas, we create strategies for obtaining customers based on a vertical focus. In the marketing world, it is essential to avoid conflicts of interest, or else a firm can end up marketing against its own client. Our business is designed in a manner that we can only represent one or two companies per industry. Therefore, it is critical for a firm to select the right clients.

We are very targeted with respect to methods for obtaining additional customers. In every account, we target how much time and soft dollars versus hard dollars we invest in getting to know a company. We view prospective clients with a year-long timeline of what it will take to develop a productive relationship.

The Challenges of Client Acquisition

It is challenging yet critical for consulting firms to inspire clients to think big. Businesses often go to consulting companies with a relatively modest project in mind that will not make a difference in the long run. In these circumstances, clients need to be shown a broad picture and taught how to consider solutions.

It is difficult enough to get clients to understand what they are buying, but when they are initially misled, this challenge becomes even more difficult. Competitors can cause problems when they misleadingly tell clients they can get something done in a short amount of time with a limited number of resources. If clients fall for their false scopes, it makes it very difficult for them to compare firms and services, because they do not actually know what they are buying. As a result, they become confused about what is really necessary to find and execute solutions.

Upcoming Opportunities for Client Acquisition

Fortunately, we work deeply within the world of digital communications and the Internet, a rapidly growing area with possibilities such as online advertising and customer management into which more and more companies are becoming interested.

Consolidation and merger/acquisition activity also affect new client acquisition. Mergers are generally used as an opportunity to survey larger companies, thus creating more work for consulting firms. It is important to recognize that merging companies may have used different firms in the past, so a firm must strive to prove itself as the better company to serve the combined entity.

The Acquisition Process

At Digitas, our industry focus and twenty-five years of history generally compel clients to target us. We receive a lot of reference accounts; our clients are very good about making introductions and generating referral business.

Once we get to know a new client, we ensure that we can foster a long-term relationship with them. This sustainability is dependent on us making sure we do not scope a project that is too big, and consistently delivering value relatively quickly. Customer service policies must be structured with clarity and managed scope.

Finding the Right Talent

Attracting and developing exceptional talent is equally as important as attracting and developing the right clients. Attracting good new hires begins with investing in the value of proposition, which is actually more important than compensation. Pay must be competitive, but it is all the training, development, and rotation plans that prove the most magnetic. Having a reputation as providing the best training ground is a critical part of the recruiting infrastructure.

As chairman and chief executive officer of Digitas Inc., David W. Kenny has led the company to become one of the world's largest marketing services organizations. Digitas is the parent company of two of the industry's most successful digital and direct marketing companies: Modem Media and Digitas LLC. Digitas companies offer strategic and marketing services that drive measurable acquisition, cross-sell, loyalty, affinity, and customer care engines across digital and direct media for world-leading marketers.

The Digitas family has long-term relationships with such clients as American Express, AOL, AT&T, Delta Air Lines, General Motors, IBM, Kraft Foods, Michelin, and Unilever.

A former senior partner at Bain & Company, the global strategic consulting firm, Mr. Kenny holds a B.S. from the General Motors Institute (Kettering University) and an M.B.A. from Harvard Business School. He is a board member for Teach for America and a director of The Corporate Executive Board.

Keys to Consulting Success

Jeff Stewart
Chief Financial Officer
Clarkston Consulting

Consulting Leadership Strategies

Success in consulting is based on two elements. The first is having a specific focus and target of what the company wants to do in the marketplace. The second facet of success is having the best and brightest people working to accomplish that goal. Finding the right talent means complimenting a very thorough recruitment process with a good internal training process.

Clarkston Consulting is a business and information technology consulting firm; over 95 percent of our consulting services are to companies within the life sciences and consumer goods industries. We employ about 250 people, roughly 200 of which are billable consultants. We've been in existence since 1991, with our headquarters in Raleigh-Durham, North Carolina.

Our company is differentiated by our very client-centric approach to consulting. We place the interests of our clients very much in front of our own, and provide a deeper, more intimate service to them than our competitors. Clarkston's culture is completely rooted in bringing value-added results to our clients, and every measure of success begins and ends with client satisfaction.

Ensuring Success

In order to expand revenues and grow profits, we have worked to be as effective as possible with our existing client base, and to establish a reputation in the marketplace as providing significant value to our clients. In any given year, over 70 percent of our revenues come from clients with whom we have done business in the prior year. Because these clients are very happy with our work, they don't want to let our people leave their facilities, and they also provide us with referrals for new business.

A professional sales and business development team is essential to growing a business and ensuring continued growth. Professional services is all about efficiently leveraging the skills of the people in the firm and maximizing their efficiency. The business development group is a critical component of that leverage, as they do a lot of the legwork required to bring in new business while not distracting our consulting workforce from the service levels needed to maintain high client satisfaction.

Challenges

I believe there are three main challenges to the consulting business. One is the general economy. There is no real driver towards information technology services right now, as there was in the past. Recently, the Internet bubble and the frenzy around Y2K brought about a surge of activity, and before that there was an enterprise push as companies realized they needed to get their house in order to integrate their systems and be more efficient. I look at the landscape today and I just don't see that general market driver out there to produce a lot of demand. That's the first challenge.

The second challenge is people. This is a very difficult profession in regard to a work/life balance, so keeping our people engaged, focused, and happy is crucial. They've chosen a demanding profession, because we are a project-based, client-focused consultancy, which means our people spend very little time in the office or in their homes. They have to be out on the job and on the road. That movement can be very hard on our people over time. As they grow a little older, they develop significant relationships that may turn into marriage and a family. Trying to maintain a healthy work/life balance while traveling up to fifty-two weeks a year is exhausting.

In order to keep our people engaged, we work closely with our clients to create flexible work structures whenever possible. Many times, our project teams are able to effectively perform the hours needed in the project by Thursday in order to attend to administrative matters from home on Fridays. We also have semiannual company meetings that we hold over a weekend. This may seem contradictory to our work/life focus, but the positive side is that we hold them in fun spots that our employees enjoy visiting, and will often bring their spouses and families. In the past, we have met in Orlando, Philadelphia, New Orleans, and Miami. Since many people in our firm work all across the United States, Europe, and Latin America, the meetings allow us to focus on our company culture, and to create an occasion when everyone can get together and have a sense of being part of a team.

Our founders formed this company on what they felt was a better model for a consulting company—one with a passionate culture about client service, employee development, and empowerment. When a person is busy working on a project out in Chicago and his or her home is in Atlanta, it is very easy to lose sight of the fact that we have a strong rallying point in our culture that binds our people together. We have to work hard to maintain that sense of purpose and teamwork.

The third challenge is keeping the "saw sharpened" as technology changes so rapidly. It is certain that very few of our consultants are providing the same services as they were five years ago, and we are continually challenged by redefining our service offerings to meet the foibles of the marketplace. It is challenging to the leadership team to anticipate where demand will arise, to prepare for it in advance, and to push our people out of their comfort zones to continually adopt new initiatives.

Keeping Our Edge

To keep our edge on a firm level, we subdivide our people into small, manageable groups that are aligned with their areas of expertise. Not only are all consultants divided into an industry focus between life sciences or consumer goods, but we specialize even further, splitting into "service lines" to further enhance our ability to meet the challenges of our clients. Grouping into service lines is important, because it bonds people who have the same interests and skills. Within those groups, they can share knowledge, and they can look over the horizon together. Actually, some of them like to say they take turns looking over the horizon, so one person alone is not charged with figuring out what the future is going to be. They rotate duties and they reinvigorate themselves, they share knowledge among themselves, they learn together, and they have a small community they can do it in. At a very micro level, we're working at knowledge management, knowledge refreshment, and keeping our edge in respect to our customer base.

Part of our company culture involves focusing on a term we call "brilliant client service," a phrase I was very attracted to when I joined the firm four years ago. It is not only about being the best and most effective, it is about being "brilliant" in everything we do. By maintaining that standard, we keep our edge both firm-wide and on a personal level. There is nothing more important in our culture than client satisfaction, and our reward system for variable compensation with our consulting force is strongly geared towards maintaining high client satisfaction. In some other firms, rewards are often based on how many chargeable hours are worked or the consultant's personal gross margin. Our rewards are based on client satisfaction and how the firm does as a whole.

Executing

We monitor how our company executes with a well-published, simple strategy based on four components.

Focus on Business Solutions

The first element is to be focused on business solutions, as technology is a very perishable commodity. The only constant in our lifetime is change, and everything changes all the time. Because of the constancy of change, we cannot be static and focused on a single technology, so we focus instead on business solutions. We are focused on providing value to our clients, and being very technology "agnostic," as we like to refer to it. It has to be the right thing to do, so we provide business solutions rather than just shove technology at clients.

Sticking to our Specialties

Secondly, we work within only two specific industry verticals: life sciences and consumer goods. We specialize to keep our focus as we remain a mid-sized consultancy dancing among the giants of the industry. If a huge insurance company would ask for our services, we would politely decline, because that industry is out of our focus. We would help them find the right business partner for their industry and keep a relationship open, but we only pursue business opportunities in our strategic verticals.

Work on a Regional Basis

The third element is to work on a regional basis so the execution of our strategy can occur on a day-to-day basis. Strategies are only as good as the people who implement them, and Clarkston's regional teams are focused on bringing intimacy to clients and consultants, as locally as possible.

Operational Excellence

The fourth strategic component is that we have adopted a culture of operational excellence. Often, consultants are considered to be like the cobbler whose children run barefoot; they promote the best business practices to the world, but their own companies are not in order. In the 1990s, we were a very rapidly developing young company with relatively little business discipline. In order to sustain our company and take it to the level we wanted, we had to adopt a culture of operational excellence. Simply stated, operational excellence is adopting those processes and systems that provide scalable controlled growth over time.

Measuring Success

I mentioned earlier that we measure success in our firm in terms of client satisfaction; that is something we take very seriously. We have the courage to measure clients' satisfaction with us as a firm, and to report those results and make improvements. The Conference Board, an independent, nationally recognized institution, conducts our annual client survey by going out and asking our clients for feedback. We also conduct internal employee surveys. Even though we have some of the highest satisfaction ratings in the industry—consistently over 90 percent satisfied over the past five years—we cannot be content, and our goal is to continually improve.

Client satisfaction is the first priority in everything we do, because without it, our business will die. As chief financial officer (CFO), I utilize many metrics to closely measure cash flow and financial performance. I compare these metrics regularly to the marketplace, and assess individual metrics by consultants at different levels. I look at gross margin by level, utilization by level, and I look at trailing twelve and twenty-four months' worth of cost levels, revenue levels, and gross margin levels. I pay attention to all the numbers, but at the end of the day, we measure the success of our business by the satisfaction of our clients, as well as the engagement and happiness of our employees. We are confident that keeping people involved and satisfied always translates into positive financial results.

Industry Changes

September 11 had a dramatic impact on the professional services industry, primarily by painting the future as uncertain. Buyers stopped spending, and then companies started planning for contingencies and grew increasingly reluctant about engaging in long-term projects. We are a consulting company working with global *Fortune* 1000 clients, and when those clients decide they don't want to embark on any major projects, that hurts us, because we are very project- and long term-focused in our sales and marketing efforts.

Another issue with the industry right now is simply that there are a lot of consultants in the world. I keep thinking it is going to change, but it doesn't, thereby driving down prices. The breakup of Andersen Consulting drove a lot of consultants into the street. However, those people didn't leave the consulting industry; they just started their own firms on a smaller basis and started competing very hard on price.

The emphasis on price is compounded by the decreasing importance placed on technology. Clients are shifting the decision-making process from the people responsible for technology over to the CFO, and are demanding a much higher return on investment in projects. This change actually helps our firm, because we've always been value-focused, and we tell our clients when we do not think the projects they envision will benefit them. We try to save money for our clients by helping them grow revenues or make operational efficiencies, which is the same as saving money. CFOs are demanding different levels of accountability for expenditures in the information technology arena.

As chief financial officer of Clarkston Consulting, Jeff Stewart is responsible for guiding the strategic financial and operational direction of the firm. He also plays an integral part in managing Clarkston's growth in the life sciences, consumer products, and industrial manufacturing industries.

Prior to joining Clarkston, Mr. Stewart served as vice president of finance at Misys Healthcare Systems, formerly Medic Computer Systems, a leading developer of physician practice management systems, clinical software, and home healthcare applications. Mr.

Stewart has been actively involved in more than sixteen mergers and acquisitions in his career, and spent almost nine years in public accounting with Price Waterhouse.

Mr. Stewart received his B.S. in accounting from the University of Alberta, in Edmonton, Alberta, Canada, and his M.B.A. from Duke University.

Over-Satisfaction: The New Currency of Consulting

Emad Rizkalla

President and Chief Executive Officer

Bluedrop Performance Learning

It may sound simplistic, but the key to success in consulting is delivering tangible value for clients. It is a simple statement, but for consulting companies that embrace it, the ramifications are profound and affect all aspects of the business. Consulting firms need to concentrate on doing something better, faster, more efficiently, or less expensively—and preferably all four—than their client can do on their own. A successful consulting company knows which of these benefits it is delivering to its clients, how the client benefits, and why it matters.

Building Meaningful Client Relationships

Bluedrop's objective when it starts a new client relationship is to become the client's "trusted advisor." We are fully committed to achieving our client's objectives, so we become a key member of the client's core team. In order to build such relationships, consulting companies must earn their client's trust on their most pressing and important issues. A good consulting company should also understand how to help the people that sometimes risk far more than their budgets by hiring them. Consultants need to speak to and address the aspirations, fears, and political realities of the people who select them. Bluedrop always strives to help the people we work with expand their knowledge, increase confidence in their decisions, and enhance their internal credibility. This is important, because ultimately consultants work with people, not organizations.

How do we build this confidence? The foundation for building confidence with a client is laid through demonstrating competence and a high degree of knowledge and capability in the area(s) with which the client is seeking help. This is why it is so critical that consultants understand how they deliver value to their clients. Demonstrable competence goes hand in hand with client education. For this reason, we strive to set expectations very carefully so clients know exactly what we are proposing and how we plan to get to the end goal.

So once a foundation of competence is established and the expectations are clearly set, there are a couple of things that are required to build and sustain confidence with clients: keeping your promises, being aware of the client's desired outcomes, and keeping the spark in the relationship.

A.   Keeping your promises: Firstly, it's very, very important to keep promises. It might sound obvious, but I believe consultants as an industry have a credibility gap in this area. In survey after survey I have seen on the wants and needs of customers in our space, vendors who "keep their promises" topped the list of criteria. Once this trust is earned, consultants must strive each and every day not to squander that trust. As the cliché says, earning trust takes a very long time, but it can be lost in a single day.

B.   Owning the client's desired outcomes: Secondly, consultants need to own the business outcomes the client seeks versus just providing the deliverables specified in the contract. Clients really appreciate a consultant that is trying to help them achieve their desired business objectives versus just finishing the deliverables, throwing them over the proverbial fence, and saying, "Good luck, I hope this solution succeeds in achieving whatever it is you were hoping for." When consultants own the business outcomes with the client, the trust and connectedness between them builds significantly as both parties are now truly working for the same common goals.

C.   Keeping the spark in the relationship: Finally, in order to build "trusted advisor" relationships with their clients, consultants need to deliver some surprises. There is an expression I heard once that "great Jazz consists of 50 percent what you expect and 50 percent what you don't." Jazz that you have heard many times before and fully expected might seem boring and uninspired. Jazz that is completely new or unfamiliar might be hard to connect with and even seem unpredictable or annoying. The same is true for good consulting, clients need to feel that their experience was a little different than what they expected or had been used to in the past. What is the 50 percent that clients expect in consulting? Things like quality and good project management are expectations, at a minimum; they are certainly not really differentiators. So often times, creating this surprise is a function of doing the "small things" that enhance the client experience. Some examples of things Bluedrop strives for to deliver this surprise include: extraordinary responsiveness; "gifts" of interesting research and industry news; delivering on all promises; providing unrelated advice when warranted and welcome; helping the client manage their internal process and needs; and holding educational sessions for staff concerning the initiative.

Achieving Over-Satisfaction

The most profitable, fastest, and easiest way to grow a consulting business is with repeat business. In our first few years of business, we focused so much on generating new clients that we missed great opportunities within our existing client base. Never again! Repeat business should form about 70 to 80 percent of revenues for a mature consulting company with single-digit annual growth.

Why is repeat business so seductive? In addition to being more reliable and having a lower cost of sale, repeat business has a shorter sales cycle time. Moreover, it is far more profitable, since you can build upon what you've already learned, and it is not necessary to go through a ramp-up curve to relearn the "terrain."

The way to generate repeat business is by earning customer loyalty, which is obviously achieved when clients are happy. To be clear, there is very limited loyalty by customers who are just satisfied. One of our mantras is to make sure our customers are very satisfied or, as we say at Bluedrop, "over-satisfied." The research says clients who are just "satisfied" are not actually loyal to their vendor(s). Only when customers move to the top end of the satisfaction scale is their loyalty assured. We focus on earning this loyalty by over-satisfying customers, which leads to repeat business within our existing accounts. Only over-satisfied customers will come back time and time again, and are not at risk of being seduced by a slick-talking competitor.

It is important to note that over-satisfying does not mean, "giving away the shop." In fact, I have found that project managers who try to "buy the love" of their clients by accepting significant scope creep actually have clients that are less satisfied than those who manage scope appropriately. In these situations, the client's expectations grow exponentially and the consultant's frustrations and zeal for the client's outcomes tend to diminish significantly, so "giving away the shop" actually reduces client satisfaction.

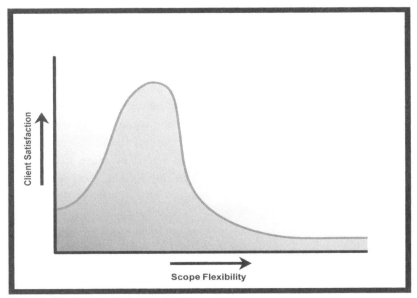

Scope Flexibility

Copyright 2004 Bluedrop Performance Learning

The graph above explains this concept. As you can see in the graph, every client will appreciate flexibility and understanding in managing the scope of a contract. So initially, client satisfaction soars with initial scope flexibility and empathy of the vendor. However, if the vendor never says "no" and is too "flexible," then client expectations will not have been managed, the perceived value of the vendor's work and time will be diminished, frustrations of the vendor team will mount, and yes, client satisfaction will actually drop off significantly.

An eternal truth of project management is that things will change immediately after the contract is signed. How consultants deal with these changes is the true test of project management. The quality of the project management response to these changes can end up determining both the client's satisfaction level and the financial health of the consulting company. In my opinion, more than profitability is lost if the consultant just ignores the contract and agrees to scope in favor of completely accommodating the client's wishes. Respect is also lost. I liken this situation to a small child who desperately gives away their lunch money in school looking to make friends. As we know, this never works.

However, the other extreme—no flexibility and sticking to the letter of the contract—is equally ineffective in building strong and vibrant relationships. So a modest amount of deviance from scope and pro bono work to help capture the top priorities of clients is the ideal way to over-satisfy clients. This deviance should be planned for and budgeted globally within a consulting company. Notwithstanding, project managers should ensure that clients are fully apprised that the changes being made are above and beyond the contract. The vast majority of clients are reasonable and understand that consultants need to make profit in order to stay in business. Clients gain respect when consultants say "no" to scope deviances as long as they say "yes" when it really matters.

Keeping Your Edge

Bluedrop's primary focus is helping clients to develop and successfully deploy electronic and blended "performance learning" content. In order to keep our edge while doing literally dozens of projects per year, there are four key elements that must be performed flawlessly: account mindset, staying current, flexible process, and continuous improvement.

A. Account mindset: Bluedrop focuses its entire team on delivering business outcomes to clients. We encourage a view of each client as an ongoing, long-term relationship versus a specific project that begins and ends. Most often, delivery-focused resources will take a project-centric view of the client, but we advocate strongly that they take a relationship-centric view. For each project, our account manager's primary internal job is to be the client's advocate and promote the vision of the client far beyond the current project. As a result, the client should feel very comfortable with the account manager, so much so that they would be comfortable calling them in the proverbial "middle of the night" with concerns or problems. The project managers are assigned to manage each project's primary objective to deliver the project to the over-satisfaction of the client. The project manager's responsibilities include delivering the project in a financially sound manner, consistent with the timelines and budgets that were established. But it is always clear to the project manager that the focus also needs to be broader than the immediate contract. The balancing act between the perspectives of the account manager and that of the project manager is the basic dialogue that ultimately keeps both clients and bankers happy.

B. Staying current: Keeping your edge and maintaining a trusted advisor status requires being very current on industry developments. It is important that senior people make time to attend industry association events and conferences, no matter how busy they are. Networking, even with competitors or other companies in the industry, is very important. We also encourage our key employees to publish one or two papers each year. Ideally, companies who want to "own the future" need to set the trends, but the vast majority of companies in any industry do not realistically have that capability. However, all companies have the capability to follow the trends closely, understand them, and adopt best practices in their industry to properly serve their clients.

C. Flexible process: To ensure that our company executes, a couple of things must happen. Firstly, repeatable and consistent processes must be in place that will always deliver the same type of quality, but not the exact same solutions. Customers don't want a cookie-cutter approach; frankly, many clients are fed up with receiving this from multinational consulting companies and smaller players alike. Customers want wisdom from a broad range of experience, but they also want solutions that speak very specifically to their needs and circumstances. So it is critical for consulting companies to have in place a methodology that arms their employees with the systems and processes they need to be efficient, comprehensive, and thorough while still providing them with the flexibility to think expansively and creatively about customized solutions for each client. Bluedrop helps our people leverage processes and experiences without constraining their creativity to deliver out-of-the-box and client-specific solutions. This is quite a juggling act, but one that clients are increasingly demanding.

D. Continuous improvement: In terms of evolving processes and methodology to achieve this balance, I think regular client feedback is the most effective way to steer it in the right direction. Companies need to regularly and formally check in with clients to ensure satisfaction and garner useful feedback. This is done through a survey, which helps the consultant know if all is working as expected, and if their systems and people are delivering value, as they should. More insight on what clients like and dislike leads to, well, more insight. So insight for its own sake is not very useful. Therefore, it is important to take all useful feedback and loop it back into evolving methodologies and processes.

Industry Change

There has been a recent shift in the value large corporations and public sector organizations place on training and its role in the success of an organization. I believe many large organizations are slowly but surely beginning to view training as an investment opportunity versus a cost center. It used to be, and still is to some extent, that training was the first thing to get cut in a budget crunch. Training was often seen as a place that organizations pour millions of dollars without really quantifying or fully understanding the benefits to the organization. A few years back, I was aghast to hear a senior executive refer to training as a "necessary evil." The good news is that now more and more executives are beginning to see training as an investment center versus a cost center. I expect this trend to grow stronger as organizations quantify the connection between increased training investment and better business outcomes.

It might seem ironic, but in the next five to ten years, there will be a continued trend towards both offshore outsourcing and viewing training as an investment center versus a cost center. Both trends are positive if consultants adapt appropriately. It is encouraging that training is moving up from a back office function into some of the executive boardrooms, and that it is often becoming intricately tied to the successful implementation of corporate strategy. This is very good news, and it's similar to the change that has occurred with the information technology industry. Twenty years ago, information technology was seen as a cost center, but now many organizations see it as a competitive advantage and an investment center. This same mindset change is happening with training. Both of these trends will fuel the demand for e-learning and redefine the roles of the consulting in providing value to clients.

Investing Where it Counts

I suspect that for the vast majority of consulting businesses, people are the most expensive asset and investment. Consulting companies have to continually invest in their people and are perpetually seeking and hiring people with talent and passion.

Once new talent is secured, it is important to train them and refine processes and standards for them to follow. This is critical for the new people to learn and enjoy their time with any company. Moreover, it is important to have these internal processes followed if clients are going to get an authentic and consistent Bluedrop experience. It is important that consulting companies put this infrastructure in place so all their people are delivering a consistent quality and client experience across vastly differing geographies, industries, and engagements.

In the consulting space, the company with the best people, and the best processes to support them, always wins. This is where companies need to invest.

Measuring and Achieving Success

Growth, revenues, and profit are obviously very important indicators of success. But ultimately, I believe companies need to measure success by evaluating the outcomes they are providing to their clients.

Repeat business is an important measure of success; if clients keep coming back, it is clear a chosen vendor is making a tangible difference to them. So in the end, I believe you need to ask yourself, "Did I really make a difference to my clients?" And if the answer is consistently "Yes," then for me, that is what defines "success." But what about shareholders, profits, and growth? Well, I have never seen any companies that can consistently answer "Yes" to this question that have not also been enormously profitable and sustained impressive growth year over year. Again, if you keep your eye on your clients' outcomes and over-satisfaction, growth and profits flow naturally. This is especially true because at the project level, it is impossible to achieve this over-satisfaction by running grossly unprofitable projects. I sometimes envision a built-in "satisfaction valve" that begins releasing accumulated client satisfaction if projects are not being efficiently managed.

So in summing up, we can summarize this section with three golden rules. The first golden rule is to measure your own success by the success you deliver for your clients. Second, you must intimately understand your clients' goals, hopes, and fears. The final golden rule is to always, always, always keep your promises.

Rewards and Challenges

Bluedrop is currently in what we define as "hyper-growth mode." This means we have been growing organically at anywhere from 50 to 100 percent each year in the last few years. Of course, this pace of growth presents many challenges, not the least of which is where a company finds the new clients to support this growth. Repeat business can generate 70 to 80 percent of a company's revenues, but not when they are growing that quickly. A consulting company that doubles its revenues year over year will need to find several brand new clients each year to sustain growth. Due to the nature of our offerings, and our desire to become trusted advisers to each and every client, the growth of our client base takes great time, money, focus, and energy.

In leading Bluedrop for thirteen years, it has been rewarding to help clients in very different organizations achieve their goals. I like the fact that this is a fast-changing industry. Where things were last year is not where they'll be this year. Everything changes very, very quickly. I also enjoy the people aspect of consulting. I don't think you can be in consulting without enjoying people—consulting generally means dealing with very smart people who constantly challenge you and push you to do more.

Avoiding Liabilities

Philosophically speaking, the easiest way to avoid a liability is to not take on projects in areas where your company and/or its people are not deeply experienced. However, life would be pretty boring if all companies did that. Most companies eventually would die if they did not get out of their comfort zone occasionally. So the keys to avoiding liability must be tied to how projects and relationships are managed.

Both the client and the consultant need to have very similar expectations, and possess a shared vision and understanding of deliverables and process. Further, the consultant's project manager has a great responsibility to educate the client on processes, limitations, and risks throughout the project. In my estimation, most liabilities occur for a couple of underlying reasons:

1. Consultants do not have the right people for the right jobs;
2. Clients are not properly educated by the consultant about the process, the consultant's costs and realities, or their own responsibilities in the success of the project;
3. Poor communications;
4. Expectations that are not clearly set, documented, and managed up front (Both parties must be on the same page of what the engagement is about, what the deliverables will be, and what the goals of the project are.)

Contracts offer relatively little protection from liability. While contracts can certainly limit damages and provide protection from unreasonable demands, justly disappointed clients can usually find some avenue for legal protest. By the time either side begins to haul out contracts and start scanning and interpreting clauses, it is already too late. The best way for chief executive officers to steer their company clear of major liabilities is to hire excellent project managers who have great processes, set up clear expectations, and educate clients. We have a saying at Bluedrop: "Project management doesn't cost, it pays." Project managers must understand exactly what the customer wants, and ensure that the client is very clear about what they will get for the fees provided. Consulting companies that do this well seldom worry about hauling out the contracts later.

Preparing for Legal Issues

Aside from avoiding the need to haul out contracts in the first place, there are several legal issues that consulting companies should keep abreast of. Consultants must strive to clearly define contracts so their liability is defined and limited to the services delivered and not to damages that may or may not come as a result. They must ensure that their role in the engagement is defined clearly, that ownership of intellectual property is clear, and that the client is also expected to produce certain deliverables (content, acceptance testing, etc.) within certain parameters and timeframes. The other large contractual issue is defining the scope of the work (and the underlying assumptions behind it) very clearly in terms of what is going to be delivered, when, and where. These responsibilities, deliverables, and timeframes should be identified for the client as well as the vendor. Sometimes, clients don't meet their obligations or timeframes; yet still expect the same timeline, cost, and effort from the consultant. Contracts need to be clear that both parties have obligations that can affect the costs, timelines, and deliverables. If not, this lack of symmetry can wreak havoc.

Keeping Informed of Legal Issues

Staying abreast of new changes in laws is a pretty organic process at Bluedrop, since we are still relatively small. Although we have clearly tasked one person as accountable for this important area (our vice president of operations), I make time for this issue in my calendar at quarterly operational meetings. I also have discussions with our lawyers and other executives at least twice a year around liability issues. Industry trade publications, conferences, and associations offer a wealth of information on dos and don'ts. You have to make sure the knowledge gleaned manifests itself in the company's contracts, processes, and methodology. Very large companies might have a whole team dedicated to this, but smaller companies tend to do it more informally, which is somewhat more risky. Bluedrop has never had a dispute go to trial or had to "settle out of court"; companies in this fortunate situation face the danger of complacency. Vigilance is important here, and that takes a conscious, concerted effort.

The legal issues that arise in our industry are typically related to breach of contract or employee grievances. To address them, consulting companies must regularly update their contracts, and identify areas of exposure in the methodology and way things are done. I recommend an annual audit by an outside consultant to ensure those processes are being properly adhered to.

Establishing and Measuring a Set of Best Practices

Before attempting to establish a set of best practices, it is necessary to network and attend industry events and conferences to learn from others.

Any company that is insular and always looking inward is not going to have the results they want when developing best practices. The very nature of best practices requires people to look externally.

It is very important to benchmark progress against corporate historical performance, as well as external industry standards. I believe consultants need to start with a vision for the client's success and work backwards to determine which internal processes and behaviors have the greatest impact on this success. Once these internal factors are identified, they must be quantified, preferably using industry-wide measurement standards. After this, companies can establish metrics to track their financial performance (efficiency, gross profit, utilization percentage, etc.) and benchmark against historical performance and industry standards.

It is important to establish a thorough client survey process to garner qualitative and quantitative feedback. The quantitative feedback is critical to benchmark progress over time. Important benchmarks should ultimately be directly correlated to employee and/or management reward programs. Client-side feedback is by far the most useful feedback any consulting company will receive. Companies have to educate the key employee groups about the new metrics, what they mean, why they are important, and how and when they will be tracked. The challenge is too often how companies translate corporate "good behaviors" into specific actions that each individual can be doing to help achieve targets.

The only reason to bother with this entire process is to use it judiciously to improve internal efficiencies and the quality of work, as reflected in a customer satisfaction index.

Tackling "The Race to the Bottom"

Some types of custom e-learning content development are becoming more commoditized. Accordingly, more and more of the low-end project work is going "offshore" to countries such as India. Of course, the costs are coming down substantially, some say by 50 percent in the past five years. This is a trend that is happening very broadly with information technology-related industries. It is one of the most formidable challenges many United States consulting companies have ever faced.

In e-learning, the client experiences with outsourcing are mixed, but I believe this trend will be beneficial overall. Lower-cost overseas providers are helping reduce the barriers to client experimentation with e-learning, and are hence creating more activity, which leads to more successes and more demand for higher-value e-learning.

Of course, clients have a right and need to do things as inexpensively as possible. The trick for the consultant is to find efficiencies without sacrificing service or quality. We have decided to take a threefold strategy to addressing this need: shifting production to lower-cost locations, leveraging technologies and tightening methodology, and moving up the food chain.

A. Shifting production to lower-cost locations: Our client service model aims to place the most important client-facing resources (such as account managers and project managers) as close to the client as possible. However, at the same time we have located our production team "near shore" in Newfoundland, Canada. In Newfoundland, we have been able to hire excellent talent at less than 50 percent of the costs associated with a major United States city. We have had graduates from Oxford, Harvard, and UC-Berkeley working there, because they were born there and wanted to return home. Our staff in such an "unconventional" location is very loyal, committed, and very happy to work with the world's leading organizations right in their hometown. Our production quality improved and our costs are half those of our competitors. Moreover, because of our commitment to hire account managers and project managers in major cities near our clients, there is no impact on our ability to build a trusted advisor relationship. Service does not suffer, quality goes up, and costs come down.

B. Leveraging technologies and tightening methodology: Another way we respond to this challenge is technology and methodology. We are perpetually looking at new technologies and tinkering with our processes to improve efficiencies. It is amazing how the latest versions of even the same multimedia software or learning content management system can shave development time by up to 50 percent over versions from just three years ago. It is critical to continuously research new technologies and products to see how they can be used to reduce costs. Moreover, it is critical to tinker often with your development processes to look for shortcuts and the removal of redundant steps. Bluedrop has taken a very aggressive definition of redundancy: any part of our process that does not add value to the client can be considered redundant. It often leaves me dumbstruck how many steps and processes devised by companies serve no tangible value towards the end goal of satisfying a client.

C. Moving up the food chain: The final response we have taken is to move ourselves up the food chain by focusing more on defining our value to clients, instead of our cost. In the current environment, consulting companies must:

1. Transition from "vendor" to "trusted adviser";
2. Reposition from a provider of "courses" or "software" to a provider of "tangible business outcomes."

Many clients will pay for value versus costs. Many North American consulting companies are shifting towards areas such as strategy, change management, high-end simulation, return on investment analysis, and program evaluation in order to shift towards the "value" side of the equation. This side is a lot more fun than being on the "cost" side of the equation, competing with companies oversees developing bulk, commoditized product. Sophisticated clients can discern when they need a "low-cost/higher-risk" production contractor versus when they should seek a "low-risk/higher-cost" trusted adviser who can deliver value. Even in the current environment, it is detrimental for consulting companies to position themselves as a low-cost provider, even if they are just that. In some cases, Bluedrop might be the low-cost provider, but I do not promote this or use this as a selling tool. Consulting companies also need to switch the equation from cost to value; that's why most clients go to consultants in the first place, whether they realize it or not.

If the only thing you can offer a client is a cheaper price, you always run the risk of being outgunned at your own game. Consulting companies need to understand the value they provide for clients and develop relationships that enhance their ability to provide it. Client over-satisfaction is the currency that consulting companies should collect, invest, and spend in the pursuit of excellence.

Emad Rizkalla is a professional engineer who co-founded Bluedrop Performance upon graduation from Memorial University in 1992. He has thirteen years of information technology and e-learning industry experience, and an additional background in marketing, organizational change management, leadership, and return on investment assessment.

In 1996, Bluedrop developed one of the world's first Web-based learning applications while assisting French Pharmaceutical, Schering-Plough. Today, Bluedrop is renowned as a company that drives the business performance through learning solutions that improve the performance of their clients' employees, partners, and customers. Bluedrop's pioneering status and track record have earned it the respect of clients such as Cisco, Dell, Microsoft, Sony, Health Canada, Dell, and Prentice Hall. Under Mr. Rizkalla's leadership, Bluedrop has grown to become one of the preeminent e-learning companies in North America.

Mr. Rizkalla is currently the chairman of The Genesis Group (the technology transfer corporation for Memorial University). He was the recipient of the Business Development Bank of Canada's "Young Entrepreneur of the Year" award in 1997, and was honored as one of Canada's "Top 40 Under 40" for his leadership and vision in May of 2000. He also sits on a task force for the Department of Foreign Affairs and International Trade, reporting to Minister Pettigrew.

Dedication: *I would like to dedicate this chapter to my wife, Laura, and the ball of energy we call Lucas. Laura, thanks for your support over the past ten years, and Lucas, "Yes, we can!"*

Acknowledgement: *Many thanks as well to Stephen Lenser, Bluedrop's director of consulting, for his "consulting" assistance. His ability to separate the written wheat from the chaff never fails to amaze me.*

Maintaining Profits and Success in a Changing Industry

Phil Friedman

President and Chief Executive Officer

Computer Generated Solutions, Inc.

How to be a Successful Consulting Firm

In the consulting business, first of all, you have to have a specialty. You have to have a product that clearly defines the markets you're going after. You cannot be everything to everyone. You have to have pickiness in the business, and you have to have very good people—experts in the industry in which you consult in—to have credibility and be able to deliver a customer's expectations.

In some respects, we are different only because, as a midsized technology consulting company, we offer a lot of different, comprehensive solutions to our customers. We call it the concept of cross-selling composite solutions. "Solutions" is in the name of the company, so with every consulting assignment we approach and get involved with, we'll look at the total solution that can accomplish the goal of the customer. We bring software sales to the table. We bring services for software, as well as technical support and training, help desk training, etc. Very few companies of our size have the capabilities to deliver a comprehensive solution today to a customer. Working with a midsized company like ours, clients get personal attention. We work with our clients on a long-term partnership. Clients see us as the vendor of choice for their entire technology strategy.

We plan in order to ensure that we are growing revenues and profits. We go through a very elaborate business process review and budget process at the end of every year, and we continually review and adjust our plans. We hire the people we need to execute our plans. We're constantly trying to develop new markets and new opportunities. The company is very opportunistic in its approach, and we think we've brought together a group of services that complement each other. So, revenues in one part of the business can pull in other revenues through the sale of other products and services.

Challenges in Consulting

Managing people is probably the biggest challenge. We pay a lot of attention to the human capital in the company, because in any consulting business, as much as we would like to think technology's important, the human capital is the most important aspect of our business. Our inventory walks out the door every night, and we hope it comes back the following morning. So turnover, staff retention, education of staff, making sure people are motivated, and making sure people are compensated for what they do, are the daily concerns in this company.

In the consulting business, the labor is the most important and the most expensive part of what we bring to the table. The labor probably accounts for 60 percent of the total cost. In our case, it's the cost of developing the products, the research and development, and the cost of labor of consultants.

Although it varies depending on the product or service we sell, we look to make anywhere from 15 to 45 percent when we sell a product. But, like I said, we have different products with different gross margin targets. Our model is to develop a profit margin that helps the business grow, but at the same time allows us to stay competitive in a market that is very price-sensitive.

Understanding Customers and Executing

We have several ways to stay on top of what our customers do and to understand their objectives. First of all, we specialize in some vertical markets where we have the main expertise, and we have experts who constantly interact with the customers. We attend seminars. We attend industry forums where we have open dialog with our customers, by visiting our customers and doing user groups. We constantly update our database, where we keep track of what's happening in our customer base. So that's probably one of the main processes. But then you read papers. You read the magazines. You understand what's happening in the industry. We look at our customers in the context of the whole industry and economy.

For the past twenty-one years, the time I've been in the business, we have a process where by the end of the week, on every Friday, the field personnel will submit a report on the progress of the company, and that will include progress in sales and marketing, and progress in delivery of our services. Over the weekend, I will read those reports, and every Monday morning, without exception, we will have a meeting of the executives of the company. And once every two weeks, we have a meeting of the top management where we review every part of our business. We see where we have problems and issues, and we deal with those on a weekly basis. We have a very well-developed process. We also have a very well-developed database where we track all the activities on every customer.

Success can be measured many different ways. First of all, financial success, obviously, is measured by financial results. And thus we keep a very close track on that. We also measure success based on achievement of strategic objectives and tactical objectives, and this is an ongoing process.

The Changing Industry: How to Keep Up

The information technology industry and consulting has changed quite dramatically over the past five to ten years. I think the industry became more competitive. There was a lot of consolidation in the industry, so you have fewer larger companies that compete. The price and quality of what you deliver are the main drivers nowadays in getting the business and expanding the business. However, it's not necessarily in that order sometimes.

You have to be able to deliver the quality, obviously. And then, every customer is looking for a competitive price. That wasn't the case ten years ago. I think the procurement departments in large corporations are getting more power and more involved; the process is more streamlined. And in some respects, I think because of procurement involvement, the process is very different from what it used to be. We used to deal with the end user more than with procurement; nowadays with large companies, procurement is a first line of defense, and the first line you have to cross before you start doing business with a company.

With these changes, we needed to change our model. We had to adjust to what's happening in the company, what's happening in the industry. We added additional products; we made quite a few acquisitions to strengthen our competitive position as a company. We then came to the conclusion that when we go to a market, we need to be able to deliver this composite solution and not be a single-product or a single-service company. We accomplished that, and that's why we stay very competitive.

In the next ten years, I think as new technologies come to the forefront, there will be further consolidation. Companies that have very unique products will prosper and companies that do the old consulting business, where they don't bring any additional value to the customer, will probably fade away.

Today, you have to be very strong, very focused, and have the main expertise in the area in which you do consulting or technical services. And again, I think there will be further consolidation in the industry. Consolidation in the market is inevitable, especially after the large technology rise in the '90s. It can be scary to see a marketplace shrink, but it also gives us the ability to maintain a position of uniqueness.

Golden Rules of Consulting

1. Listen to the customer.
2. Always deliver on what you commit to.
3. Be sensitive to price pressures and competitiveness in the marketplace.

Creating a Successful Consulting Arm

First of all, you have to have a very strong sales and marketing message, and you have to have name recognition and a brand in the vertical market or the space in which you're trying to do consulting work. Then marketing programs, a very strong sales team, advertising, and so forth can support that, but you have to have name recognition in the industry if you want to be successful.

Number two, you have to have very strong domain expertise. You have to be recognized as a leader in some very well-defined space, where the customers will come to you because you have a unique expertise in a vertical market, or unique expertise with a product or set of services. That should be what differentiates you.

Number three, you have to serve your customers. You have to deliver quality. You have to make sure you live up to the commitments you make to the customers.

The ability to develop a domain expertise where you can bring additional value to the customer and to make sure the customer recognizes the value you bring are two of the most important things in consulting. If you can create a return on investment to the customer, I think you can charge higher fees. The customers will be happy to pay the fees if they appreciate or understand what your consulting generates for them.

What makes us different? Number one, we're still an entrepreneurial, fast-moving company. We make decisions based on what we see in the market; we don't go through a long, bureaucratic process. Number two, we have a very solid and good set of products and services we bring to the market. And number three, we deliver on our commitments to our customers.

Keeping Up

Frankly, I don't see much flawed with consulting today. You have a lot of relatively small companies trying to get into the space with no depth and expertise. And if they fail, sometimes it gives a bad name to the industry, or give a bad name to the field. But generally, I don't see anything terribly wrong with consulting today. Smaller companies often tend to be most aggressive on price. However, we see that those who are too aggressive most likely fail in the end, as their business model is not well-structured.

Companies need to be able to constantly relocate what they do and adjust their process to make sure they're not falling behind on technology. They have to constantly reevaluate their go-to-market strategy and probably reinvent themselves every eighteen months.

Challenges in Consulting

The challenge is to deal with perception; the challenge is to convince the customer you have their best interest in your heart, and develop this trust from day one, where the customer will open up, embrace you as a partner, and really include you in the decision-making process.

This will probably take time if the customer had a bad experience. There's a lot to overcome with that. You have to prove you bring a lot of expertise to the table and that you have the best interest for the customer involved.

It's mainly a human relations issue. It's a communications issue. It's reporting. You have to agree up front how you will inform the customer, and what the best way is to communicate to the customer. It has to be an ongoing process where you relate progress to the customer and get feedback, and constantly adjust the process as needed as you go along.

The opportunity in a situation like this is to show the customer every kind of investment, and show the customer that, based on what you are delivering, the customer will do better and see benefits of your deliverable.

The Changing Landscape of Consulting

As part of our process, we are constantly interacting with our customers. We are implementing customer service. We are further expanding our user confidences. We are constantly sending out newsletters to inform our customers on the progress of the company. So we're improving communications, we're soliciting feedback, and we act if we have a problem. We tackle problems head-on and resolve them in a timely manner.

We are expanding our business on all fronts, but we have a brand new product called Unlimited Mailbox, which is an acquisition we made recently, and we believe this technology will be a dominant technology in e-mail storage and archiving.

Unlimited Mailbox is a product that allows companies to retrieve e-mails without having them stored in a main server or on the PC. So to the user, it's visible at any time; the user sees it as if it would be stored on his or her personal PC, where in fact it's being stored on a tape drive storage device on a backup server that is not clogging the main system infrastructure of the company.

Right now, with Sarbanes-Oxley and with requirements to save e-mails for seven years, a lot of companies have major issues with retrieval of e-mails. Beyond the efficiency, storage costs on these types of archives can be tremendous.

With our solution, we can cut down on cost of storage; we will make it available on demand. Instead of storing a hundred copies of the same e-mail, we store only one. So it cuts down on the cost of storage and makes it immediately available to anyone in the company who is entitled to see it. This product is a new opportunity for us in the marketplace. Beyond the unique offering it provides, it opens doors for more long-term consulting engagements. Once we introduce our strong list of competencies to the clients, they often want to work with us as a partner to uncover additional projects to improve their business processes.

We are also expanding our consulting business around portals, and portals for some vertical markets, specifically in the medical and legal fields. We see a major opportunity there. Companies are looking for ways to streamline their business processes. They look to a technology solution and our strong expertise as the logical fit to develop and implement the solution.

Additionally, today we are the number-one solution provider in the fashion industry and the technology industry. We feel this part of our business will start growing very rapidly. Our product is an ERP solution that currently has gained tremendous traction in the fashion industry, but in reality is an optimal solution for any discrete manufacturer. We are starting to provide solutions for companies outside traditional apparel and footwear, and are working with companies that provide accessories and home furnishings. We anticipate that this product will grow at least 30 percent in the next year and the upside beyond that continues.

Phil Friedman was born and brought up in the post-World War II Soviet Union. After spending twelve years in different positions in the electronic industry, he emigrated to the United States and settled in New York. In addition to his degree in electrical engineering, economics, and finance, Mr. Friedman acquired a degree in information systems from New York University.

In 1984, after eight years in various positions within the information technology industry, Mr. Friedman started Computer Generated Solutions (CGS), a leading provider of system integration, software, training, and managed services to businesses and government agencies worldwide. Today, CGS is an international company with presence in twenty major cities in the United States, Canada, and India.

On several occasions, CGS was recognized as one of the fastest-growing privately held companies in the United States by Inc. *magazine and Deloitte & Touche. In 1996, Mr. Friedman was named "Entrepreneur of the Year" by Ernst & Young,* Inc. *magazine, Merrill Lynch, and the city of New York. In addition to his day-to-day management of CGS, Mr. Friedman sits on the board of directors of the services division of the Information Technology Association of America.*

Understanding Client Needs and Delivering Results

Doug Gorman
Chief Executive Officer
Information Mapping, Inc.

Selling Consulting Services

The main consideration for building a successful consulting business is to package and sell a suite of consulting services that identifiable customers need to improve their businesses/organizations. In execution, you have to exceed the delivery expectations you set, and you do that by setting up an expectation where you make sure you can at least slightly exceed what you've told the customer you were going to do. You must help the customer see the value of what you told them you were going to do, and what you actually did. Often, there are multiple layered benefits to your work that you can help the client to understand.

Different from most consulting companies, we have built a dedicated sales force that focuses on selling our services, and the sales force has only a minor role in the actual delivery of those services. We use "solution selling" —our sales force diagnoses a customer's problems, and how those problems affect their business, and then we bring in a senior consultant to talk about the proposed solution. This way of selling works very well for obtaining new customers. Once we have a customer with a successfully completed engagement, the salesperson may transition into the role of an account manager with some of the actual selling performed by the senior consultant who led the project. For a senior consultant to gain a commitment for additional work is largely based on the confidence the client has in the consultant and the work completed. This split between new sales and additional sales to existing clients works well. In the prospecting process, salespeople are much better at dealing with the level of uncertainty and rejection experienced in the process of attracting new clients.

A consulting company can generate growing revenues and profits through a well-constructed incentive system. Since we want to connect specific performance outcomes with people's job functions, the structure of incentives varies by job function. We have incentives based on revenue for some people, based on gross margin (which we define as revenue minus the cost of delivering the service) for others, and based on contribution margin (which is revenue minus the cost of delivery, minus all the other expenses of the specific consulting business) for others. Virtually everyone in the organization has an incentive that is tied to some metric. Of course, we cannot have revenue and profit growth without satisfied customers. We are confident that anyone on our customer list would say we are a good company to work with and that we deliver real value. This kind of reputation, supported by incentives, ensures growth in the long run.

If there were three golden rules for success in any consulting business, they would be:

First, be clear about expectations so you can deliver—under-promise and over-deliver. In the IMI/customer partnership, we work hard to ensure good communication about what we are going to do, what we expect from the client, and what the specific deliverables and milestones will be. Second, have one person manage the project, including responsibility for delivery and pricing of the project, so they own the delivery at a certain cost and we have received their commitment to a project plan. We want our project managers to be responsible for meeting both client satisfaction expectations and our internal financial metrics. Third, don't work with customers you don't trust, or who don't seem to trust you. There are organizations that try to maximize the resources (as opposed to value) they get from an engagement without regard for the effort required by the consultant to deliver top-quality work. In the end, the customer must be happy with the deliverable, our company must make a profit, and our people must feel good about how they are treated by both our company and the client. Our experience has shown that if the client and the consulting organization cannot form a strong partnership in the early stages of the relationship, the project and the relationship will ultimately fail.

Challenges of Consulting as a Commodity

What we sell is very conceptual—better organizational performance from better information. But the quality of information is almost never "owned" by a C-level executive. And while a company might have budgeted for technology, or improving sales or compliance, nobody budgeted for improving the quality of information. In fact, rarely do our customers connect the impact of their poor information with the business performance metrics they see every day. Yet, every knowledge worker and executive knows at some level that their information is inadequate for the varied needs of their employees. Therefore, we have to sell something that's very conceptual—better information—and try to make it as concrete as possible for the customer—specific results. To do that, we try to understand the customer better by having them describe their business challenges and goals, and we do not assume we understand them on our own. Some customers will perceive quality problems, and some will say they have a performance problem. The common thread for us is the need to get better information to people so they can do their jobs. In the end, what we deliver may be similar. It's better design of information, and better information. We try to meet the customer where he or she describes the actual pain, and whatever it is that's keeping them awake at night.

We have a view that almost any issue in a company has three dimensions: a people dimension, a technology dimension, and an information dimension. To solve a problem, whether it is a strategic or a tactical one, there's usually an element of getting somebody motivated and getting them to do the right thing—the people dimension. There's usually an element of technology—how information is going to be delivered, or how they use technology. But ultimately, there's also an element of whether that information is accurate and accessible—is it described well to people, do they understand what they're supposed to do, when they're supposed to do it, how they're supposed to do it? Our consulting practice focuses on improving content, or the information itself, to solve the broader organizational problem.

In consulting, it's important to be able to develop a knowledge advantage with respect to your customers' issues and your solutions. We need consultants and executives who are continuous learners. Face time with an executive is one of the best ways to develop this knowledge advantage— just talking about their job and what the issues are. I learn a tremendous amount every time I talk to a customer about the problems they're trying to deal with. I'm also a voracious reader—I read a lot of magazines, business magazines, *Newsweek*, *Time*, *Fortune*, business newspapers, and trade publications. Reading and face time is how I keep in touch with the business world. I also consult various research reports and track key industry trends.

Measuring Your Performance Success

How does a consulting company know if it is executing successfully? Simple —if the customer isn't happy, you haven't executed well. And if the job goes way over what you've budgeted, you haven't executed well. It may be obvious, but if your client will not be a reference or will not refer you to other colleagues, then you have not executed well.

We keep our eyes on the money and where we are in a project to anticipate sudden problems that will take us over budget. And we try to, as early as possible, determine why we've got a problem with the money in an engagement. Is it that we haven't executed well? Or is it that assumptions have changed? Are we delivering something different than what was agreed upon at the start of the engagement? We put financial controls in place. We measure revenue growth, profit growth, and then we look for repeat customers. A repeat customer is a sign of a happy customer and a successful execution.

Another indication of an execution problem is when, during the consulting engagement, the client becomes difficult or adversarial, and simple issues become battles. Timing is critical, as you need to work with the customer to understand what happened, and why. This is a good time to leverage the senior management of both organizations, and successful resolution of these issues can actually create a more positive long-term relationship.

A Changing Industry

The information explosion has dramatically changed our industry. In the beginning, people tried to deal with the information explosion by attempting to read more, read faster, and cast a wider net. It is now clear to everybody in the consulting business that you just can't keep up with everything. So, I think we have to deal with getting both our employees and our customers enough information to do their jobs without overwhelming them with too much unusable information.

People's attitudes and thresholds for taking action and getting things done have also changed. Ten years ago, people would initiate programs because they thought something should be done for a probable payoff sometime in the future. Now, they seem to be focused on only what they absolutely have to do, or what's absolutely going to generate an immediate return on their investment. The nice-to-haves don't happen in today's economy.

The involvement of lawyers and the level of legal review that we see has increased. Both the level of internal policies, and the complexity of contracts required for us to do work, have changed. All public companies must comply with Sarbanes-Oxley. To comply with Sarbanes-Oxley, organizations need to document what they do and how they do it. No part of the organization is untouched, and legal and compliance officers are regularly involved in various decisions—even simple ones.

The Executive Position in Consulting

Rewards

For me, a leadership position in the consulting industry has many rewards. I have had the opportunity to work with intelligent, interesting people and to develop a positive culture. In the past, I've seen companies, and been in situations prior, where people mislead employees and customers in order to make money. I've come to the conclusion that every company is made up of three partnerships: a partnership with customers, a partnership with employees, and a partnership with shareholders. Each of those partnerships has clear responsibilities. It is not just a one-sided philosophy of what we owe our customers, our employees, or our shareholders—they owe us something in return, too. That makes it a partnership. When it works, there are many monetary and psychic rewards.

Challenges

With all its rewards, leading a consulting business has its challenges, too. At the top of that list is working with the customer so they understand and budget the amount of money needed to do the job right the first time. Also, recognizing the complexity of the information environment in which most people and companies operate is somewhat of a challenge to the leadership of those organizations. And then, the most recently appearing challenge is dealing with the increasingly empowered legal and purchasing environment.

Client Communication

Consultants and clients can best communicate by not being afraid to address issues and asking the hard questions right off the bat. How is this really going to work? What happens if this happens? The sooner you can have those conversations, the better, and you can have them much easier when they're hypothetical than when those things have actually happened. You can also have them more easily if you are consistently open and communicative.

A lot of times, we are in the position of helping the customer avoid a mistake, and it's often difficult to measure the value in that. If we prevent a company from being sued, it's impossible to measure how much it would have cost them had they been sued. So, how do we prove our deliverable has measurable value? Even though the customer can't see the value of getting the right information in the beginning, in the long run, they can see it, and that needs to be discussed. How much time are they spending actually looking for information they could find more quickly, thereby increasing productivity? How do you quantify that? People at all levels seem to understand that they waste time looking for the information they need, and they often find information that is inadequate.

Every customer wants a big return on their investment in technology, products, and services. In our experience, you can usually make the numbers show a positive return on investment, but ultimately, both you and the customer have to feel in your gut that there was a significant positive payoff from a service.

Preventing Potential Problems

Client Management Issues

Working to get on the same wavelength with a customer about how to solve problems is really a communication function. Get to know the company and the people in it. Get to know what makes them tick, and what they do for their customers. It's a relationship, and mutual expectations need to be both set and met. Ask questions like:

- What are we going to do, and what are you buying?
- What does "goodness" look like?
- What does "complete" look like?
- What will make you look great?

It's important to avoid laissez-faire project management—if somebody isn't managing the job to the numbers and the client expectations, there will be trouble. Often, a less-experienced project manager, left to him or herself, will think their job is to give the customer everything they ask for throughout the project. But that's wrong—his or her job is to deliver everything the customer asked for in the beginning, when the consultants first signed up for the project. Sometimes, the project manager may forget what his or her responsibility is, either to their company or to the customer company, because he or she is the one that has to walk the line.

Payment and Legal Issues

Another issue the leadership must deal with is customer payment. A customer who isn't paying is a problem. A situation like that cannot be ignored for long, because after the customer hasn't paid for two or three months, the problem becomes insurmountable. The best practice is to set the customer payment terms up front, and make sure everyone understands the terms. Non-payment usually indicates an issue that needs attention.

We try to address legal and purchasing issues directly with top-level business people. We try not to get turned over to the lawyers; we try to have the lawyers work through their business people, and the result is usually a more reasonable contract and mutually agreed-upon expectations. Often, with consulting, we are presented with a contract that was meant for buying products, or software, and that kind of a contract makes no sense at all for our business. Clients must understand that they really are buying a service, not a product. Steer clear of major liability commitments in the consulting marketplace.

Almost all engagement begins with an analysis phase. At some point, there is generally a written work product. There must be agreement on how long it is going to take the customer to assemble and communicate comments to the draft deliverable. This may seem simple, but it is crucial to dig in and ask, "Could you tell me how you are going to turn the comments around?" "Who are you going to give it to?" "How many people are going to look at it?" "Are you going to have ten different people give us comments? Or, are you going to have one person consolidate all the comments?" Misunderstandings here can greatly affect the cost of doing the job.

The key to successfully meeting any of these challenges is constant, regular, and direct communication within the context of the customer partnership.

Doug Gorman has led Information Mapping, Inc. (IMI) since 1986. During this time, he has created an organization and positive culture that has permitted IMI to thrive.

From the classroom to the boardroom, under Mr. Gorman's leadership, IMI has been transformed from a think tank to a thriving commercial entity. IMI has built upon its research-based methodology and products to help its customers solve real-world information-intensive problems across industry lines. IMI focuses extensively on the pharmaceutical, financial services, petrochemical, manufacturing, telecommunications, and government markets, where it has developed significant long-term relationships.

IMI has developed an international network of customers, strategic alliances, and partnerships in more than thirty countries that has positioned the company for continued, sustainable, long-term growth. The company offers seminars, consulting, and software services to help its customers improve the creation, access, use, and maintenance of mission-critical information.

Mr. Gorman has been honored as a finalist for Inc. *magazine's "Entrepreneur of the Year" award, and IMI has been recognized as a finalist for the Greater Boston Chamber of Commerce "Small Business of the Year" Award.*

Mr. Gorman has a B.A. in psychology from Colby College and an M.S. in management from MIT.

Acknowledgement: *I would like to thank the leadership team of Information Mapping—Steffen Frederiksen, Dan Morgan, Tom Raleigh, Debbie Kenny, Susan Spark, and Bill Ferguson—for their commitment to Information Mapping and the excellence they bring to our customers on a daily basis.*

Meeting the Challenges
of the Consulting Industry

Carla O'Dell

President

APQC

Offering Functional Processes

Success in consulting is dependent upon the ability to offer an improvement methodology that actually works. If the process implemented by a consulting firm can produce results, the firm will gain the client's trust. However, if a consultant fails to get results, then all he or she had to offer was very expensive sound and fury. It is essential to our success and our reputations as consultants that we be able to add value to people, both as individuals and as professionals.

Our three-part mission is to discover and define organization and process best practices, broadly disseminate what we learn, and create networks of people who can learn from each other and are interested in particular bodies of knowledge. APQC's research agenda—performance, process improvement, knowledge management, measurement, and benchmarking —supports this mission, and we accept consulting work that is consistent, in turn, with our research agenda. Therefore, our consulting and change initiatives are primarily related to our mission and are not processes we employ simply to create revenue. APQC is mission-driven, as opposed to profit-driven, and that makes a big difference in terms of how we select clients and projects.

During our projects, we build in extensive training and co-delivery with our clients. We co-design the strategy and methods, based on APQC's knowledge and experiences with best practices and the client's deep knowledge of their organization. We train them by both formal workshops and by having them work with us on teams. APQC seeks to interact with clients, empower them, and positively impact their performance. By truly collaborating with our clients, we share our experience and knowledge with their employees so they can continue after APQC has completed the project. Unlike many consultancies, APQC does not typically work on engagements where a large APQC contingent remains on site for years. Instead, our philosophy is fundamentally different. One analogy we use is teaching people how to fish, rather than fishing for them. APQC professionals strongly believe in sharing and transferring knowledge so all organizations improve performance.

Challenges: Selling and Data

Many consultancies struggle with "porpoising," as revenues rise and dip, which occurs when a consulting firm becomes so involved in delivery that they forget to sell. As a result, when a project ends, the firm has to scramble to find a new project and a way to generate revenue. Overcoming this challenge requires that research projects are sequenced in such a way that those highs and lows can be avoided. APQC has other sources of revenue, such as memberships and consortium studies that help smooth out this porpoising cycle.

Another challenge of this business is obtaining data. People frequently do not take surveys correctly, or are too busy to take them at all. Therefore, gathering data is an expensive and time-consuming process. We must sift through the millions of organizations worldwide in order to find those that need our product and are ready to contribute their performance data. Then we have to court them through the process of actually providing that information so we can produce research reports that will benefit the participating organizations. This entire task of finding, gathering, and analyzing data constitutes an incredible amount of work that does not directly generate revenue.

Through years of benchmarking research, APQC has developed a proven methodology for benchmarking organizations, which truly is collecting data. Using this methodology, APQC has spearheaded the Open Standards Benchmarking Collaborative (OSBC) research, which is the overall effort to develop commonly used processes, measures, and benchmarks that are available to organizations worldwide to improve performance. The mission of the research is to establish, lead, and promote a universal process framework and performance metrics, created by industry for industry. The OSBC research strives to enable rapid and innovative improvement within organizations.

Led by APQC and the project's advisory council, this global research will identify performance levels within key business, government, healthcare, and educational processes. The measures the research will focus on are cost, quality, cycle time, and productivity. The research will also deliver tools organizations can use to embrace standards around processes and measures.

To gather data that will be used in this research, APQC has built an online database (www.apqc.org/osbcdatabase) that collects organizations' performance data and keeps the information confidential. Once organizations have submitted their performance data, APQC experts validate the data for accuracy and provide each participating organization with a customized performance report that compares its processes to top performers and other relevant peer groups. This allows management teams to know where weaknesses exist and where they should focus their improvement efforts. It's a finely-tuned process for collecting data and packaging the information in a useful way. Plus, as a nonprofit, APQC provides this benchmarking services at no charge, whereas other organizations provide similar services for tens of thousands of dollars.

Keeping Informed

It is important to constantly listen to the voice of the customer. We do consortium studies in which twenty to forty companies come together to perform research while we are physically with them discussing what they want to learn. By doing about fifteen of these consortiums a year, we can obtain a tremendous amount of information about the state of the market and the businesses with which we work. We also create online surveys that help us understand member organizations' concerns and needs.

Dozens of people are employed at APQC to collect data and analyze it so we can know what does and does not work. An engine of knowledge creation is constantly running (e.g., consortiums, OSBC research, and custom research), and it is our duty to study it ourselves in order to keep our own personal knowledge up to speed. Sharing this knowledge helps APQC meet its mission of identifying best practices and disseminating that information with organizations globally. By sharing this knowledge, APQC helps all organizations improve performance.

Industry Changes

The consulting industry as it is known today did not exist twenty-five years ago. It sprang up and experienced an enormous bubble of growth that culminated in the dotcom bust. Organizations were hungry for the external perspective and tools consultants could bring, and especially the information technology advances of the last two decades.

Currently, information technology is still a major driver of every key business process. It has changed consulting staffing, pricing, methodologies, and the duration of projects. This emphasis on technology will continue to have an impact on the consulting industry in the years to come. Furthermore, global integration will become a paramount issue in the next ten years. China will become a big market for consulting, and many growth resources will be concentrated along the Asian Pacific Rim.

Ensuring Success

A high-powered team of people coupled with a strong accountability system and performance measures are the keys to APQC's successful business execution. Once these elements are in place, it is also important to keep an eye on customer satisfaction—whether through after-action reviews or debriefing sessions—in order to ensure that the work is actually effective.

Standard financial measures serve as a reasonable means to monitor success. APQC also uses other measures, such as a project pipeline of requests, cost management, and customer satisfaction as general leading indicators of what will be reflected financially.

We continually train and share knowledge about leading practices so our potential clients come to us for best practices and data they can use to drive their own improvement.

Ultimately, the most critical elements of successful consulting go back to having a process that works, delivering results, and being trustworthy.

The work of Carla O'Dell and APQC in the area of knowledge management dates back to 1995, when APQC conducted the nation's largest symposium on knowledge management, with more than 500 attendees. In 2002 and again in 2003, APQC was selected as one of the "100 Companies that Matter in Knowledge Management" by KMWorld Magazine. APQC is also a proud winner of the 2003 and 2004 North American Most Admired Knowledge Enterprises (MAKE) award.

The thrust of Dr. O'Dell's current work is knowledge management and sharing of best practices. Under her direction, APQC has become a national leader in conducting and producing knowledge management best practice consortium studies, publications, and training. She has most recently finished The Executive's Role in Knowledge Management, *with Paige Leavitt, published by APQC publications in 2004.*

In 1987, Dr. O'Dell designed and led for APQC the largest national study ever conducted on innovative reward systems. The study of 1,600 firms employing more than 9 million people still serves as the benchmark study in the field.

A popular keynote speaker at senior executive events, Dr. O'Dell frequently appears on business television. She holds a bachelor's from Stanford University, a master's from the University of Oregon, and a doctorate in industrial and organization psychology from the University of Houston.

Leading by Example

Mark Agustin

Senior Vice President and Chief Financial Officer

STI Knowledge, Inc.

Understanding Customers and Developing Solutions

One of the fundamental keys to finding success in the consulting field is the ability to thoroughly understand all aspects of the customer's business. The key ingredient to success is employing experienced and knowledgeable consultants who can build relationships and serve as true business partners throughout all levels within their customer's organizations. Consulting firms and consultants must be extremely proficient at quickly assessing areas of weakness, formulating solutions, and communicating such solutions to the customer in a manner they can understand, readily integrate into their company's operation, and use to quickly materialize value for their shareholders.

Through clearly understanding the customer's business, we can then determine a proven methodology of how they can get from their current state to their desired outcome. Often, consulting firms provide solutions that attempt to "boil the ocean" and fail to yield clear and executable corrective action plans that lead to successful outcomes for the customer. In order to "cure the disease and not just treat the symptoms," it is essential to effective consulting that we develop solutions on a micro level to attack and eliminate the customer's weakness at the root cause level.

Differentiating in the Marketplace

At STI Knowledge, we differentiate ourselves from other consulting companies by offering a multi-phased approach. We decompose the consulting lifecycle into three defined phases: assessment, implementation, and certification and compliance. During the assessment phase, we compare the customer's current state against our set of industry-recognized and adopted customer care best practices to determine where the opportunities for improvement exist. The STI best practices have been developed over ten years of on-site customer care and consulting engagements. Having this assessment methodology in place lends credibility to the work we do in both consulting and outsourcing. The final assessment report gives the customer some instant deliverables and value that can be implemented at the moment the report is delivered.

By offering a clear roadmap from our assessment, we can then concentrate our efforts during the implementation phase on executing the service principles and business processes to achieve the desired best practice productivity improvements. The value in this phase of our approach is not only the immediate process improvements, but also the ongoing measurement and monitoring to drive sustainable results. An example of this phase of our consultative offering is our action plan which provides step-by-step improvement recommendations utilizing our customer care best practice methodology to achieve best-in-class performance within your enterprise support function.

The third phase of our consultative approach focuses on certification and compliance. Utilizing STI's industry-recognized and adopted certification curriculum, we incorporate training programs designed to drive complete adoption of the consulting solution. All of STI's consulting solutions also provide a framework for ongoing monitoring and evaluation against best-in-class metrics. By setting the bar high for both quality and effectiveness, the customer is better prepared to provide validation of the true value of the support organization.

Our goal at STI is to provide process solutions that allow our customers to deliver their products and services to customers in more efficient and cost-effective ways. In order to continue to meet this objective, in addition to our unique valued-added approach to consulting, STI clearly differentiates itself through our ability to offer customers a turnkey outsourcing solution. In many cases, after successful consulting engagements, we may offer to manage the customer's business process, function, and/or operation on an outsourced basis. This gives customers additional options for savings through our onsite, onshore, offshore, or blended shore delivery and support model based on their business, economic, and risk needs and goals.

Although our consulting practice is a small piece of our organization, it is critical in terms of maintaining our thought leadership position in our target industry sectors. In this highly competitive environment, it is important that we demonstrate our expertise while expanding our offering. As a smaller company, obtaining access to a large and well-established company can be challenging. But the credibility we have been able to build through our consulting practice has proven critical to overcoming this challenge.

Our people, process certification, and methodology, combined with industry-specific tools and technology, are the core assets of our company. It is where we invest a significant portion of our growth capital. Our fundamental value proposition lies within our ability to leverage our experience and industry domain expertise. The tools, technology, and process certification and methodology help customers reduce cost, increase productivity, and improve quality within their organizations.

Keeping an Edge

In order to ensure that we stay abreast of new developments, we employ subject matter experts who work to keep pace with the never-ending changes in our target industries. Approximately 65 percent of our business is in the healthcare vertical. In terms of the mix, 80 percent of our healthcare practice is focused on the payer space and 20 percent is in the provider space. We have subject matter experts in both the payer and provider segments, obtaining information we use to produce internal curriculum, training, and certification programs for keeping our people current with the latest legislative, operational, and regulatory changes.

Our company is recognized as the industry leader in education and certification within our customer care enterprise support industry. We are able to remain leaders in this area because of our extensive knowledge base and industry-adopted best practice methodology. Our customers look to STI to stay current on changes within this industry sector. We have trained and certified over 25,000 customer care knowledge professionals, representing over 75 percent of the *Fortune* 100 companies.

New Developments in the Consulting Industry

The very dynamic environment of the healthcare industry provides the greatest challenges for our customers and a unique opportunity for STI. The fragmented nature of this industry lends itself to greater risks due to the number of changes occurring within each of the segments. HIPPA is the largest of these developments, but there are other issues pending through upcoming legislation. On the payer side, which mainly includes large insurance companies, third-party administrators, and self-insured health plans, I believe margin pressures combined with more regulatory compliance will force payer companies to look at cost-effective alternatives to improve the efficiency and effectiveness of their back office operations.

On the provider side of healthcare, I believe similar pressures will prevail and force hospitals and physician practices to seek better ways to manage their back office support functions, and I expect technology changes to play a major role in these initiatives. For example, hospitals will look to service providers that can provide cost-effective solutions to improve their revenue cycle management metrics. By implementing best practice methodology and best-of-breed technology, providers will improve cash flow and collections, so they can focus the majority of their efforts on quality patient care. The increasing demand for these services align directly with STI's core offerings, and will provide a tremendous opportunity for us going forward, both in terms of consultative services and outsourcing solutions.

I believe technology will continue to play a significant role in how consulting firms deliver their solutions. By understanding the customer's business practices and processes, we can provide improvements through automation by leveraging industry-specific enabling technology that can integrate easily with other mission-critical business applications. This will enable us to provide our services much more cost-effectively and drive immediate results. The technologies that enable us to work remotely and utilize the internet to its full advantage allow for greater flexibility to operate at customer locations and deliver projects, reports, data, and more.

Success Going Forward

Success for consulting companies going forward will consist more of the same formula—maintaining a thought leadership position within your target industry domains and leveraging that position to build and sustain business partner relationships with your customers. Maintaining a deep understanding of the customer and utilizing that expertise to help improve the business practices and processes they deploy to provide products and services to their customers, as well as keeping them on the forefront of changes in their industry and competitive landscape, are essential to future success.

I also believe the ability to educate customers on how to leverage offshore resources as a cost effective and high-quality alternative for the transaction- and administratively-intensive functions within their operations will be a critical success factor.

STI continues to invest a significant portion of its growth capital to further develop and strengthen our knowledge base within our target industry sectors. With our recent acquisition in India, STI now has high-quality, cost-effective global delivery capability it can offer to our customers based on their economic objectives. In the next eighteen months, our goal is to deliver over 60 percent of our effort from our offshore facilities. The key for STI will be educating our customers of the economic, efficiency, and quality benefits they will gain through our offshore and blended shore delivery solutions.

Mark Agustin is the senior vice president and chief financial officer for STI Knowledge, Inc., and has served in this capacity since joining the firm in March of 2003. Mr. Agustin is responsible for STI's financial strategy initiatives and for ensuring operational excellence that results in sustainable profitability for the company. Since joining the firm, Mr. Agustin has been instrumental in helping the firm successfully through three rounds of equity funding, raising over $39.5 million in venture-funded capital.

Before joining STI Knowledge, Mr. Agustin was senior vice president and chief financial officer of Coastline Distribution, a national wholesale distribution company. During his tenure, Coastline increased profit margins and reduced debt by over 500 percent and 70 percent respectively. Prior to that, he served as vice president of finance for IMRglobal, a publicly traded global information technology services provider. Mr. Agustin was instrumental in helping IMRglobal complete ten acquisitions and grow revenues in excess of 40 percent. Prior to IMRglobal, he held senior financial management positions with large, publicly held global organizations, including stints at ADP and Dixons Group.

Mr. Agustin holds a B.S. degree in business management and accounting from Widener University.

Key Strategies for Growing Your Business

J. Wayne Gudbranson
President and Chief Executive Officer
Branham Group Inc.

Succeeding in Consulting

Our firm, established in 1990, is a Canadian-based, globally directed, go-to-market strategy consulting company targeting the information technology industry. Our work is project-specific and aimed at the executive level in organizations worldwide. Although based in Canada, 70 percent of our revenues are from non-Canadian clients, about 75 percent of which comes from the United States, and the rest of which comes from Europe. We provide services to established and emerging brand name information technology vendors from small to large cap. We do everything on a custom consulting basis, which clearly differentiates Branham from the volume sellers of over-the-counter reports. We help executives make informed decisions about the short- and long-term future of their businesses.

A number of factors contribute to quality consulting. Subject matter expertise and knowledge is, of course, one factor. We, for instance, focus exclusively on the information technology and information communication technology businesses. We don't veer off into any other jurisdiction. Our employees have worked in the industry and love it, which is important.

Not only do we target the information technology industry, but we also focus our effort on assisting the vendors of products and services. We help these vendors understand how to grow through marketing innovation. I think that really sets us apart. We don't provide consulting services directly to the users of technology as of yet.

Second, we have developed a series of approaches or methodologies to help us deliver value to our clients. This value is exhibited in our commitment to deliver statistically meaningful market data and analysis, and actionable recommendations.

Third, we hire people who have a combination of business and information technology knowledge. We find the combination of marketing and technical skills works well for us. We also employ people who, by their nature, love multitasking. This is important, because working in a high-paced consulting practice means never really working on just one assignment over any given twelve months. Working on multiple assignments for multiple clients is not uncommon, so a successful consultant has to love that variety and has to be comfortable with the speed at which things must be done. Again, we work with companies that need input right away to help them deal with tactical and strategic issues in the marketplace. So, those are the three key components to success—sector focus, proven methodologies, and great people.

One more element we feel sets Branham apart is that we are a custom consulting operation. We fundamentally feel every client's requirements are unique. Given that an executive's mandate is to constantly improve the performance of their business, they are also faced with market uncertainty. They need answers to a multitude of unique questions. Only a customized project approach can generate the data they need to make informed decisions.

Generating Growing Revenues and Profits

There are three mechanisms to encourage revenue growth at Branham. First, Branham has deployed a major account or name account strategy. Effectively, we generate roughly 70 percent of our annual business from regular customers. In this business, you are only as good as your last project, so you have to do really well on every project to continue that account relationship. Every year, we generate 30 percent of our revenue from new accounts, which may be one-project situations, or they may morph into longer-term accounts. Our core strategy, then, is to build tight, integrated relationships with vendors to generate a reasonably predictable annuity revenue stream and profitability.

Second, given our custom consulting delivery model and our focus on selling to the executive level, we find the best marketing to be word of mouth. The most powerful communication vehicle in this case is the high quality of our work.

Third, there are certain economic advantages to being located in Canada. It effectively allows us to offer high quality at internationally competitive rates. Our customers, as a result, receive considerable value.

Challenges

In the consulting business, we face numerous challenges. First of all, the information technology sector is prone to market demand fluctuations. One of the factors that cause low demand is the inability of end users to absorb new technology at the pace at which the vendors can produce it. This creates a problem of unused inventory. Ultimately, this can create market complacency by the vendors, which can generate a reduced demand for outside advisory services.

Another challenge in the consulting business is the ability of clients to absorb research and analysis into their decision-making process. This fundamental inability to incorporate external input into the decision-making process can create a lack of demand for our services. This is a challenge.

At the core of everything we do is market research. Quite simply, our research and analysis provides informed input that, when properly used, can reduce risk in growing a business in the fast-paced information technology sector. However, the challenge for companies like Branham is respondent weariness. Quite simply, organizations and individuals within are reaching survey exhaustion. Our industry must demonstrate, more than ever before, creativity in our ability to capture the salient market information. At Branham, we are constantly looking for innovative ways to address this ongoing challenge.

Finally, we live in a time of immediacy. We must have everything "yesterday." This contemporary societal behavior pattern does permeate all walks of life and business, including the consulting business. But the consulting business is a very human-intensive and intellectual pursuit. Good research and analysis requires time—a commodity that appears to be in short supply sometimes. So this is another challenge we must overcome.

From a purely business point of view, one of the challenges in the business is managing expenses. I realize this is a challenge that is not necessarily restricted to the consulting industry, but there are unique traits in this sector. As I mentioned above, consulting is a very human-intensive and intellectual endeavor. One can always research and analyze a market sector ad nauseam. But, unless one manages expectations, "scope creep" can take place and have disastrous effects on your profit margins. In reality, any consulting business must achieve a ratio of two and a half to three times the employee cost model to ensure solid revenue growth and profitability.

Keeping Your Edge

We do a number of things to maintain our competitive edge. Given that we work with vendors, our internal team is tasked with monitoring the performance of various vertical and horizontal markets (i.e., players, new products, trends) in addition to the revenue-generating consulting work that is conducted. Effectively, this is our research and development expenditure. We also endeavor to provide relevant training to our team of consultants.

We also have strong processes (i.e., project management, consulting methodologies) in place to make sure our company executes well and that our team delivers on time and within budget. A major part of maintaining our competitive edge, however, is retaining good quality people. If you don't have the right kind of people, you won't deliver.

Measuring Success

Financially, we have all the metrics in place to review our revenue and profit lines on a month-to-month basis, which is one way of measuring success. We also measure success in terms of retaining our customer base. If a customer comes back and hires us to do another project, that's a very good indicator. However, it should be noted that satisfied clients don't always come back for another consulting engagement immediately.

Another measure of success involves the development of new accounts. As I mentioned before, we annually identify vendors we would like to capture as new accounts. There is always a little attrition in our account base each year, and obviously we like to replace outgoing clients with new ones. We also endeavor to monitor new accounts that are known versus emerging brands.

Given that Branham is a focused SMB player in the consulting segment targeting the information technology sector, we do endeavor to track our success in scooping clients from our competitors. This is another way we measure success.

Changes in the Industry

In the last five to ten years, the meteoric changes in technology and its rapid adoption has been both a positive and negative experience. Years ago, industry pundits used to talk about how the use of technology would change lives for the better. We would have more time to effectively "smell the roses." Well, these promises haven't really materialized in some respects. Yes, of course, there are vivid examples of where archaic processes and procedures have been changed, such as banking and accessing information, but I fundamentally believe technology has accelerated the pace of life so we are at times numb to its experiences. We have created a world of instant gratification. People never seem to appreciate what they produce or receive, because they are on to the next challenge.

My father-in-law, for example, ran a very successful worldwide consulting civil engineering business for thirty years. He managed several multimillion-dollar engineering projects around the world. But I can recall him telling me about the impacts of the fax machine when it was first introduced. No one questioned its convenience, but what he noticed was that it accelerated the pace of work rather than make it more enjoyable. His colleagues became more anxious, and the expectation for instantaneous feedback increased. Effectively, people have reduced the time needed to appreciate their efforts.

At Branham, we work in a global market. Technology has fundamentally enabled our team to work in a virtual environment wherever and whenever, and it has allowed us to be responsive to our customer needs on a 24/7 basis. Five years ago, this was not the case. But, although technology has allowed us to be more flexible with our time, it has created an expectation, both market- and self–induced, that we are always "available." Our team uses devices such as the Blackberry extensively. These devices are incredible technology tools, but it is also difficult to turn them off. We have to be careful that we don't become slaves to technology.

From a market research industry point of view, the climate is changing. We live in a time where organizations and individuals question the value of participating in industry surveys. It is incumbent upon our industry to continue to identify and develop innovative ways to engage respondents. This is where technology can play a major role.

Golden Rules

The consulting industry is like no other. Where else can you work with several different clients on a myriad of different assignments and have a meaningful impact? But, given the reliance on human intellectual capital, it is an industry that consumes you. It's an industry in which you are only as good as your last project, and you are always thinking about the next project, but one golden rule is sacrosanct: You must deliver on time and within budget. Failure to do so erodes brand equity and profit margins quicker than a snowflake in a heated oven.

Best Practices for Growing Your Business

Our strategy for growing our business is twofold. As a custom consulting shop, our focus is on addressing the unique requirements of our specific clients. We build on the experiences of each project to fine-tune our capabilities so we can improve our delivery with the next client. We have learned to turn information into knowledge.

Second, we are also augmenting our custom consulting revenue with a series of multi-client studies that focus on emerging information technology opportunities. The scope of these projects is typically larger than any one player will fund, so we sell this research to a plethora of vendors. The most recent initiative is a review of current and future use of ICT in the healthcare sector. In this case, we have elected to focus on the Canadian market initially. Our subscribers to this project include known international brand names, emerging companies, government organizations, and industry associations.

So these two business streams—custom consulting projects and multi-client studies—will continue to grow. Remember that 70 percent of our business is from outside of Canada, that our marketing approach is to connect with executive management teams, and that our large focus is the markets of North America, Canada, the United States, and Europe. Occasionally, we do work in Latin America. So we will continue to go after established and emerging brands in the information technology vendor community.

On the International Playing Field

From the beginning of Branham in 1990, our strategy was to go global. In fact, our first accounts were global. We fundamentally believe Branham is a better player, because we compete on a global scale with the United States, Europe, and other firms. There is also another reality for a Canadian player like Branham—the domestic market is simply not big enough. A Canadian company has to seek export opportunities to increase revenue and keep abreast of industry developments.

International Challenges

We have encountered very few challenges working in the international marketplace. The biggest issue, really, is understanding different cultures, business practices, and regulatory environments. In the international business environment, value is more important than geographic origin of a supplier. Our clients want the best possible strategic market advice.

Legal Issues

Legal requirements are always a concern. We are cognizant of regulatory and legislative requirements like Sarbanes-Oxley, for instance, in the United States. We respect those requirements as we work into different countries.

Operating Internationally

You need a separate set of best practices for each country in which you operate. Having said that, I should add that we don't. As previously indicated, our success is largely due to the people, the subject matter expertise of those people, and the methodologies they employ. Those apply regardless of geographic boundaries. Again, typically we deal with businesses that are global in orientation, so we don't necessarily dissect our approach or come up with radically different approaches country by country. Having said that, the market of Canada is quite different from the market in the United States, and that is quite different from the market of Germany. But this is more of a knowledge understanding as opposed to a different set of best practices.

Clients want to know to what extent we have worked internationally, names of previous clients, the size of those projects, and how successful we've been. Clients also want to know to what extent our results had a positive impact on that organization. They also want to know to what extent we are accessible and available on an international basis.

Analyzing Areas of Growth

We have an in-house target to achieve two and a half to three and a half times multiple on the salaries within our organization in order to maintain our targeted profitability. That's how we manage our business. In terms of identifying areas of growth, I task each of Branham's employees with the responsibility of not only retaining existing clients, but also expanding our work within these accounts. Given that 70 percent of our annual revenue comes from regular clients, this is very important. We measure performance on a project-by-project basis and by contribution to bottom line.

Investing in a consulting industry is radically different from investing in other businesses. Consulting, more than any other business, is a people-based business. Your greatest resources are your people and the subsequent subject matter knowledge and skills they offer. We don't see nor expect a return on our investment in a new employee for the first six months, despite the varied richness of their previous experience. We typically team new employees with someone who has been here longer, and we gradually move them into a scenario in which they can play a more pivotal role.

Using Consulting as a Means for Growth

Achieving growth can be very challenging. It requires an unwavering commitment to tactical (short term) and strategic planning (longer term).

At Branham, we find that a lot of organizations do not have rigorous strategic and tactical planning processes in place, and therefore many of them are constantly in a react mode to the market. When there is strong market growth, many organizations become complacent — effectively lulled into believing their companies will continue to do well. They run the risk of assuming change is not required. This mentality can sew the seeds of potential market demise in the future.

So, we believe there is a need for organizations to respond more proactively by putting structured planning processes in place that will enable them to establish a path for continued growth. This is where a firm like Branham can be utilized effectively. We can establish the planning framework and facilitate the planning processes in an objective manner.

Growth in the Next Twelve Months

In the next twelve months, there are several areas we believe will impact growth in our firm. First, we will focus on helping organizations effectively use our outputs in their decision-making processes. Given that information technology vendors retain Branham to effectively help them reduce risk and improve their go-to-market success, we have to make sure our outputs are directly aligned with critical decisions. The market is moving so quickly that clients need to understand that so they can adequately make decisions about their business.

Second, Branham will expand its business beyond our traditional custom consulting capability into other areas such as multi-client studies. There are a number of market studies we believe information technology vendors collectively support.

Making a Profit in the International Marketplace

The best ways for a consulting firm to make a profit in the international marketplace is to focus, specifically target, and own a niche. We are exclusively focused, for instance, on the information technology industry and, specifically, on vendors. So we understand this market very well. If you focus in that regard, you will do very well, and that's the first step towards achieving revenue and good profitability. The minute you go beyond that, you jeopardize, to a certain extent, your potential success, and that requires an investment. So given that consulting and consultants are intellectually-oriented, they are constantly taxed with coming up with intellectual deliverables; if you've focused into one key area, that's great, and you're able to leverage your knowledge, which is important.

Profit Areas

In a people-intensive business like consulting, profitability can only be delivered by managing client expectations very closely, and delivering the output within the agreed budget and time frame.

However, any annuity stream business you can get is certainly one of the most profitable areas of consulting. For instance, we regularly prepare and distribute competitive analysis reports to major information technology vendors' companies. These reports are not widely published, but are targeted to specific clients. We have perfected the process of delivering these products, allowing Branham to effectively increase its margins.

J. Wayne Gudbranson is president and chief executive officer of Branham Group, Inc., an international information technology strategy and marketing consulting firm. An information technology industry strategist, Mr. Gudbranson actively advises many of the established and emerging brands in the global information technology industry. He has been instrumental in launching and re-launching companies and/or products in Canada, the United States, Europe, and other parts of the world. Mr. Gudbranson has an encyclopedic knowledge of key players in all segments of the information technology industry and an extensive network of senior contacts in the global information technology sector.

Mr. Gudbranson established Branham in 1990 and has since successfully built the company into a world-class go-to-market consultancy providing planning, marketing, and partnering services to global information technology companies. From its base in Ottawa, Canada, Branham now consistently generates over 70 percent of its business from markets outside of Canada.

In addition to directing Branham consulting services to global information technology companies, he has been a passionate promoter of Canada's information technology industry capabilities. He has been invited to speak about Canadian information technology capability in more than twenty-five countries around the world, from Norway to Costa Rica, from Japan to Germany, and from the United States to Mexico. Eleven years ago, he launched an ambitious initiative to raise the visibility of Canadian information technology companies with the Branham300 project. The Branham300 is the most comprehensive database of privately held and publicly traded Canadian information technology companies ranked on total revenues. In 2001, he launched another ambitious effort to recognize excellence in the Canadian information technology vendor community. The Branham Awards is a semiannual premier awards gala that brings together Canada's information technology executive elite to celebrate the industry's success.

Mr. Gudbranson has an honours B.A. from the University of Guelph and an M.A. from the University of Western Ontario. Prior to establishing Branham, Mr. Gudbranson worked for Canada's leading software company, Cognos, Inc. He resides in Ottawa with his wife and four children.

Dedication: *To my wife, Donna, and my four children, Erik, Alexander, Dennis, and Chantal. Also to my colleagues at Branham Group, Inc.*

Success Is the Only Option

Steve Bloom
Chief Executive Officer
PRAGMATEK Consulting Group

Positioning for Success

"Success is the only option" has been PRAGMATEK Consulting Group's mantra since opening our doors in 1991. As a niche player in the management consulting field, hiring the right people is key to what we say and do as a business. Consultants are our "products." That's why we engage what I call a TEC model during the interview process to examine people's talents, experience, and their potential to fit into our culture. This cultural fit is imperative for boosting employee morale and client relationships. A candidate may have the moxie, requisite experience, and the ability to perform the job, but personality-wise and culture-wise they must fit in with PRAGMATEK internally, based on our business model, as well as externally with our client base.

Given that every consulting firm's "product" is their people, a second success factor is differentiation in the marketplace. Our sales and marketing messages focus on how PRAGMATEK uses specialized value-chain skills to drive business improvements and optimize SAP systems as demanded by today's C-level decision makers of middle market, American companies. Unlike large national accounting firm consultants, we provide an individualized, customer-intimate, and highly responsive service that creates extraordinary results, yet also enables clients to replicate the improvement process themselves.

The third essential component for success is a high degree of customer satisfaction. Without it, consulting firms have little ability to get to the next engagement and grow profitably. To gauge effectiveness in this arena, customer satisfaction surveys can examine performance related to meeting deliverables, staying within the scope of the project, and adhering to budgetary and time constraints. Tracking performance data and maintaining a continued effort to improve upon these key indices allows consultants to build credible references for use in selling their next engagement.

In short, my Golden Rules for positioning our success are:

- Hire the best.
- Find a way to differentiate yourself from your competition.

- Treat success as the only option. Do everything possible, internally and externally, to satisfy your customers and employees.

Consulting Leadership Strategies

As a consulting business, there are three strategies we focus on: return on investment for our clients, sales growth, and consistent progress towards our goals with our clients.

First, we focus more on a project's return and less on its cost. Hence, we help our clients up front—before we even engage with them—in understanding the scope of the project and how time and cost relate to ROI. This approach is driven by a strong focus on management consulting and process improvement services. If clients know that they will spend $250,000 over twelve weeks with PRAGMATEK, and they will save over one million dollars in one year as a result of implementing our recommendations, they usually don't focus on the initial investment.

Another key element of any successful consulting company is good salespeople and processes, which directly grow the business. In this regard, we follow a solution-selling process. This begins by addressing clients' needs and pains—not explaining our service offerings. With this approach, we don't just talk about what we're going to do for them but rather, we pinpoint the key areas of their business where the most improvement is possible. By focusing on the issues they face and where opportunities lie to decrease their business costs, we are able to compete more effectively in the marketplace. Once we have found the areas where we can create value for our clients, we position our services within that context.

Consulting is performance-based, so the third aspect of our approach is measuring progress with our clients using an account plan. For every ongoing account engagement, we track performance against promises as well as other possible opportunities where we might help the client improve. We assign client partners to each account to ensure we are meeting the client's needs and living up to preset expectations. If done properly, this system drives higher utilization of our existing consultants, and a strong sales pipeline as future projects are identified for each client.

After every engagement, we then perform a customer satisfaction survey to further track our performance.

At the end of the day, our success comes down to our sales pipeline, profits —the types and utilization of our staff—and customer satisfaction. We track these areas closely and if our sales pipeline is X, our utilization and profitability is Y, and our customer satisfaction rate exceeds 95 percent, then we are successful.

Internal Review & Performance Metrics

Organizationally, we have a constantly evolving, goal-oriented program titled "The Success Plan," which covers three core areas: sales growth, maintaining a performance-based culture, and keeping our service offerings up to date.

For example, our latest plan for the upcoming quarter outlines strategy for sales growth, including geographic expansion, adherence to the sales plan, and marketing initiatives. This strategy is based on our vision to be a dynamic, nationally recognized business improvement and SAP solutions provider. In addition, we look at forecasting accuracy for our sales pipeline, bookings, schedule revenue, anticipated revenue, bench report (available consultants), and recruiting pipeline. We also track our sales pipeline with our worldwide business partners—IBM and SAP.

When reviewing our goals around a performance-based culture, we look at each employee's contribution on a quarterly basis. We measure his or her contributions as it relates to teamwork, flexibility, client satisfaction based on job performance, and demonstrations of leadership. We also review our communication plan, developed at the beginning of the year, in order to create better relationships between the field and office/sales personnel and overall awareness in the marketplace.

Finally, with respect to services, we review our current offerings and how to improve them in order to continue to bring value to our client base. We keep in mind that our mission is to help clients realize significant productivity gains and increased profitability by applying process improvement techniques and optimizing SAP business systems. We have an internal team of consultants who are constantly reviewing and improving our service offerings as well. This program, called IGNITE, takes into consideration what training and coaching our staff will need in order to deliver services to our clients. This also helps in defining career paths for our employees. Following "The Success Plan" helps us execute on the tactics for achieving our goals.

Measuring ROI

Of course, ROI is a big factor in determining whether a project makes sense to undertake. To evaluate ROI with respect to a consulting investment, prospective clients should consider gauging whether the investment helps to reduce costs and determining if it helps to increase revenue. Remember, you're either saving or growing — but either way you're making gains.

To ensure one of these objectives is achieved, PRAGMATEK uses industry proven metrics to continuously gauge how the client is doing with respect to each of its business segments. We use a "scorecard" to rate the supply chain's efficiencies, for example. In examining the different aspects of the supply chain, we identify benchmark metrics to gauge efficiencies and determine areas for improvement. On the sales side, we use a similar "scorecard" for gauging the demand chain that deals with all the metrics relating to increasing revenue within a client's business.

Consulting firms are highly capable of measuring ROI as it pertains to their clients' businesses, but for the firm internally it can be a bit more challenging to do so or perhaps it sometimes goes overlooked. Consulting companies, PRAGMATEK included, are so focused on getting the engagement and making sure the engagement is successful that they lose track of whether or not it was a good investment for the company. This should carry equal importance when considering a deal.

For clients and consulting firms alike, achieving the greatest cost savings is about looking at the major cost centers within the business, breaking them down by metrics, and determining where the biggest opportunities are for cutting unnecessary spending.

Greatest Challenges

Being strategy-focused and goal-oriented does not eliminate all of the challenges within the business. When consultants are not engaged with a client for forty hours a week, it causes a heavy burden on profitability. The consulting business all boils down to the consultants because, as the "product," they make up more than 70 percent of the cost. It is challenging to keep them fully utilized. If a consultant is not fully utilized, wasted hours can never be regained.

It is extremely difficult to find the "right mix" in terms of having enough resources available to staff engagements that are about to start, without having too many consultants not billing and reducing profitability. Striking this balance is a huge challenge. It requires a highly accurate sales pipeline as it relates to the probability of a particular sale closing. In addition, it's imperative to know when consultants will be ending a project and available for new work. Finally, the recruiting pipeline for new consultants has to be full, accurate, and reviewed to enable hiring any consultants needed to meet demand if not enough current employees are available to perform the pending work.

Another difficult aspect of the business is creating a performance-based culture. Most good consultants worry first about the customers and tend to forget about the internal organization in which they work. We put a focus on serving the internal organization, PRAGMATEK Consulting Group, by setting aside 10 percent of the net profits for the year into a bonus pool. This bonus pool is distributed to employees based on how well they have served the firm including leadership, attending internal events, speaking and writing engagements, attending training to improve their skills, and any other activities that improve the company.

The third most challenging part of the business is good communication. This is difficult given the fact that in consulting, most of the employees are remote. Everyone is not in the same facility on a consistent basis; being able to connect consistently, clearly, and thoughtfully is imperative. The use of well-planned technology and monthly gatherings helps improve the effectiveness of communications.

Keeping Your Edge in a Changing Industry

A constant challenge, which is really more of a necessity, is staying ahead in the business—keeping a finger on the pulse of the marketplace. To this end, I established an advisory council about eight years ago, which consists primarily of former and future clients. Within that mix, there is also industry expertise—people both inside and outside of our business who might have more of a sales or marketing background, as well as small business owners. We meet quarterly and spend much time talking about what these individuals believe is coming next in terms of future developments, business issues, industry trends, and most importantly, where they and their customers will be spending money for business improvement.

The Y2K crisis had a tremendous impact on the consulting business. It enabled a multitude of people to enter the industry and help clients to position themselves for greater profitability. At the same time, it spurred enormous demand across the country to meet the needs of so many clients. There were not enough consultants to handle the Y2K demand, which led to an expansion of the consulting industry and a dramatic increase in business and profits for those positioned to take advantage of it.

Yet, the Y2K boom came and went. Once the need was met for compliance, many companies went out of business, merged with others, or downsized. Now, five years later, the need to update business systems again is resurfacing. Companies are looking to upgrade applications, streamline operations, and improve and integrate their operations. Thus, the industry is starting to pick back up again.

The good news is that there are fewer competitors relative to the Year 2000. Even so, larger consulting organizations are starting to realize how they need to readjust the type of business they go after to remain dominant. In the past, some firms sold only to Fortune 500 or Fortune 100 companies, which, of course, limits the number of prospects. Consequently, these firms are now playing to middle market companies as well as those whose revenues might range from $100 million up to a billion dollars to stay on top. With fewer, more competitive players today, differentiation is critical for success.

The answer, in part, is for consulting companies to focus on industry and sector specific solutions. At most, companies are picking about five industries, focusing on understanding their needs, and conceptualizing solutions to meet those needs. This is drastically different from the situation even five years ago when companies often offered services across a broad spectrum of industries.

Companies have given up trying to be "all things to all people," so there are many more strategic partnerships within the industry. In the past, partnerships were convenience-based, but today there is an additional element of strategy coming into play. For example, PRAGMATEK is now fulfilling IBM's needs for SAP skills generated by their clients in the small- to medium-sized marketplace. In return, IBM has a window of opportunity for selling to the middle market clients where PRAGMATEK has an established presence and track record.

Trends for Garnering More Revenue

One of the major areas where consultants will help clients to win more revenue over the coming years is SKU rationalization. This process involves looking at how many customers the client actually sells to, asking them to identify their top customers and what they do for them in terms of pricing, promotion, and service. Depending upon the customers' varying levels of commitment to the client, appropriate service levels can be established in the interest of weeding out some of the less dependable customers and focusing on, for instance, the 20 percent of customers who provide 80 percent of revenues.

Another key area in the coming months is product lifecycle development. This is how clients examine the length of time and costs for bringing new products to market. Even if a product is not widely accepted, it can still be considered successful if it is introduced to the marketplace in a specified period of time at the right cost. Similarly, companies should look at their ROI when a product is widely successful and accepted by the marketplace, in terms of how much was invested—in both time and money.

For most companies, technology can be instrumental for a few processes becoming more and more essential. The ability to implement a good customer relationship management (CRM) application helps a company to stay close to customers while tracking how accepting they are of new products. It indicates who is buying which products, in what quantities, and at what price. Anything that helps clients understand their customers and cater to them is indispensable for their continued success.

Missed Opportunities

For all of the possibilities management consulting poses, there are a proportional amount of missed opportunities. Consulting should begin with addressing problems, not focusing on implementing new technologies for the sake of technology itself. Approaching a problem in this way often helps to justify the costs required in order to make a project successful. Technology has to be a logical solution for fixing a particular problem or meeting a specific end.

But the key to ensure that opportunities with consultants are not missed is reviewing the project weekly—with executives from both companies in attendance—and this rarely happens. Management needs to be at the table to review, update, and adjust the project accordingly. Both sides need to understand what is happening, what is going well, and where things can be improved. In the end, this ensures higher degrees of customer satisfaction and adds value for all.

Steve Bloom started his career as an IBM marketing representative before joining PRAGMATEK Consulting Group in 1991 as vice president of marketing. He was appointed president and CEO in 1996 and became majority stockholder the following year. During his tenure at PRAGMATEK, Mr. Bloom has grown the organization from seven employees and $250,000 in revenue to over a hundred employees and $22 million in revenue. One of his key business strategies is developing partnerships with major industry strongholds, including SAP America, IBM, and the Supply-Chain Council. Mr. Bloom is most proud of the culture that makes PRAGMATEK such a great place to work. He has co-founded two other businesses in the technology and entertainment fields, in addition to a family-owned business that raises show-caliber llamas for profit. In 2002, he was one of the original founders of Social Venture Partners/Minnesota, a nonprofit, philanthropic organization dedicated to addressing *local children's issues using a venture capital model. Mr. Bloom's motto in life is "If you can't burn the candle at both ends, don't light it."*

Dedication: *I would like to acknowledge Susan Blakely for her writing support.*

New Releases

- <u>HR Best Practices</u> - Top Human Resources Executives from Prudential Financial, Northrop Grumman, and more on Hiring the Right People and Enhancing Corporate Culture - $27.95
- <u>Staffing Leadership Strategies</u> - Best Practices for Working with Customers - $27.95
- <u>The Art of Consulting</u> - Gaining Loyalty, Achieving Profitability, and Adding Value as a Consultant - $27.95
- <u>CEO Leadership Strategies</u> - Key Methods and Traits for Business Success - $49.95
- <u>CEO Best Practices</u> - Skills, Values, and Strategies for Successful CEOs - $27.95
- <u>International Public Relations</u> - Successful PR Techniques for Use in Major Markets Around the Globe - $219.95
- <u>Inside the Minds: Public Relations Best Practices</u> - Industry Insiders Offer Proven Tips for the Most Effective Communications Strategies - $27.95
- <u>CMO Leadership Strategies</u> - Top Executives from ABC, Time Warner, and More on Creating and Delivering Successful Marketing Campaigns That Impact the Bottom Line - $49.95
- <u>Sales Leadership Strategies</u> - Top VPs on Increasing Sales and Inspiring Your Team - $27.95
- <u>Getting Your Message Across</u> - IR and PR Executives Offer Leadership Strategies and Keys to Success - $27.95

Management Best Sellers

Other Best Sellers

Visit Your Local Bookseller Today or visit www.Aspatore.com
for a Complete Title List

- <u>Ninety-Six and Too Busy to Die</u> - Life Beyond the Age of Dying - $24.95
- <u>Technology Blueprints</u> - Strategies for Optimizing and Aligning Technology Strategy and Business - $69.95
- <u>Being There Without Going There</u> - Managing Teams Across Time Zones, Locations, and Corporate Boundaries - $24.95
- <u>Profitable Customer Relationships</u> - CEOs from Leading Software Companies on using Technology to Maximize Acquisition, Retention, and Loyalty - $27.95
- <u>The Entrepreneurial Problem Solver</u> - Leading CEOs on How to Think Like an Entrepreneur and Solve Any Problem for Your Team/Company - $27.95
- <u>The Philanthropic Executive</u> - Establishing a Charitable Plan for Individuals and Businesses - $27.95
- <u>The Golf Course Locator for Business Professionals</u> - Organized by Closest to Largest 500 Companies, Cities, and Airports - $12.95
- <u>Living Longer Working Stronger</u> - 7 Steps to Capitalizing on Better Health - $14.95
- <u>Business Travel Bible</u> - Must-Have Phone Numbers, Business Resources, Maps, and Emergency Info - $19.95
- <u>ExecRecs</u> - Executive Recommendations for the Best Business Products and Services Professionals Use to Excel - $14.95

Call 1-866-Aspatore or Visit <u>*www.Aspatore.com*</u> *to Order*